THE PAT METHENY INTERVIEWS

THE
PAT METHENY
INTERVIEWS

THE INNER WORKINGS OF
HIS CREATIVITY REVEALED

BY RICHARD NILES

Pat Metheny in conversation with Richard Niles

With contributions from Gary Burton, Lyle Mays, Mike Metheny,
Jack DeJohnette, John Patitucci and Jay Azzolina

Edited by Ronny S. Schiff

Published in 2009 by Hal Leonard Books
An Imprint of Hal Leonard Corporation
7777 West Bluemound Road
Milwaukee, WI 53213

Trade Book Division Editorial Offices
19 West 21st Street, New York, NY 10010

Photographs on pages xviii, 2, 3, 4, 6, 21, 28, 38, 43, 46, 57, 78, 93, 111, 114, 116 and 144 are from the private collection of Pat Metheny.

Photographs on pages 44, 55, 64, 96, 102, 115 and 121 appear courtesy of Ted Kurland Associates on behalf of Pat Metheny.

Printed in the United States of America.

Book design by Mark Lerner.

Library of Congress Cataloging-in-Publication Data
The Pat Metheny interviews : the inner workings of his creativity revealed / by Richard Niles.
     p. cm.
  Includes bibliographical references and index.
   ISBN 978-1-4234-7469-2
   1. Metheny, Pat–Interviews. 2. Jazz musicians–United States–Interviews. I. Metheny, Pat. II. Niles, Richard.
   ML419.M477A5 2009
   787.87′165092–dc22

                              2009029032

www.halleonard.com

CONTENTS

CONTENTS

CONTENTS

CONTENTS

PREFACE

Pat Metheny is one of the most critically acclaimed,
commercially successful and musically significant artists
of the last fifty years. His career is one of unparalleled
achievement including over thirty albums, innumerable
awards, three Gold Records and seventeen Grammys. But
then you probably know all that already.

This book is based partly on interviews I did with Metheny
for BBC Radio 2 in 2007, plus many other interviews on
several other occasions. I was producing, writing and hosting
a three-part radio series titled *Pat Metheny—Bright Size Life*
broadcast by the BBC. The title was slightly misleading
because although I had "pitched" the idea to the BBC as a
bio-documentary, I had no intention of wasting anyone's time
talking about Metheny's well-documented (one might say "not
secret") life story.

PREFACE

I have been fortunate to know Metheny since 1974 when I was in my third year at the Berklee College of Music. One of my teachers, the great vibraphonist Gary Burton, told me that an incredibly talented young guitarist was joining his group, and he had given Metheny a teaching job. A small number of students were chosen to study with Pat Metheny. How I, with my limited technique, was chosen for that lucky group of people, I don't know. I can only assume that Burton felt it would benefit me as a composer. As in all other musical matters, he was right!

The gigs* Metheny did in Boston clubs and bars were literally shocking. None of us had ever heard anyone play any instrument the way he played his (even then) slightly battered Gibson ES175. More significantly, we had never heard anyone play music like that before. He was so impressive that the fact that he was performing with superb talents such as Jaco Pastorius, Bob Moses, Steve Swallow, Mick Goodrick and Danny Gottlieb was almost an afterthought!

My fellow students (who included the great guitarists Mike Stern, Jay Azzolina and Mitch Coodley) and I were aware that fueling this creative maelstrom were Metheny's surprising

---

* A gig is a commonly used word to denote a paid musical engagement. (N.B. There is no specific expression to describe an *unpaid* musical engagement—which is surprising considering the fact that, for most jazz musicians, this is unfortunately more common.)

maturity and volcanic focus—at the age of nineteen. Since then I have seen that same focus in a few of the artists I've worked with—Ray Charles, Paul McCartney, James Brown and Michael McDonald.

An artist is his own work of art. He creates like a sculptor, subtracting the irrelevant to leave the essential. Faced with a block of marble, Michelangelo removed material until what was left was the statue of David. Bringing together selected disparate elements of mainstream jazz, country, Brazilian and rock music, and purposely deciding NOT to do other things, Metheny created something fresh and unique. The result is impassioned and highly personal yet universally accessible.

How an artist achieves this is fascinating, and in these pages Metheny is articulate as he explains his methodology. But what had always interested me about artists who are inspiring was to discover what inspired them to do this work. Not so much the "how" but the "why."

One question was: Where did the dedication and obsession come from? I lived in a house with Metheny for a short time in 1975. Why would a person begin practicing as he woke up, continue all day long with the briefest of meal breaks, gig until one A.M., return to his room to practice a couple more hours, sleep a little and do the same again, every day?

Another question was: Why does a person develop a unique concept? Yes, he loved Wes Montgomery, Jim Hall, Bill Evans and Miles Davis. But despite his love and respect for the traditions of jazz, Metheny revolutionized both the guitar and jazz. I don't know if the question is strange or obvious, but I want to know: *Why?*

What was the character and creative sensibility that enabled a kid from Lee's Summit, Missouri to become one of the most important artists in the history of jazz? Although the public only sees the end result, the recordings, the concerts and the awards are only the facts of Metheny's accomplishments. Here he reveals *why* he was driven towards music with a stratospheric drive and dedication—even as a preteen. You'll view the inner workings of his creative mind, seeing step by step how he set and achieved each of his own demanding goals.

Fortunately, Pat Metheny answers questions in a manner so articulate that people who don't know him well often look around to see if he's using autocue!

I have known Metheny for a very long time: as his student at Berklee, as his host whenever he'd drop in for dinner, as a producer and colleague in the studio and as a friend for over thirty years. So in this book, he's talking to someone who he's comfortable with, someone who would rather discuss his philosophies than his amplifiers and string gauges.

I also asked questions *beyond music* because I know that underneath all that charisma, theoretical knowledge and dynamic talent there is the intense philosophical mindset that created it. Pat Metheny is more than a bunch of cool notes that are fun to listen to. There is a nexus in his brain where Clifford Brown meets Nietzsche and they discuss nuclear physics while playing the changes to "Stella by Starlight"!

The interviews have been edited only for reasons of clarity. They are interrupted by a few explanatory notes and some comments from some significant people in Metheny's life.

As the saying sort of goes, "a few notes are worth a thousand words." With that in mind, I asked Metheny to demonstrate his concepts and methodologies on the guitar, and I have transcribed those unique performances for those readers who want to "play along with Pat." For those of you who can't read music, this book may make you want to learn!

ACKNOWLEDGMENTS

My heartfelt thanks to Pat Metheny, both for making himself available for these interviews, and for speaking with the same creativity as his playing. My special thanks to Janek Gwizdala, Christine Donald, David Sholemson and Ronny Schiff for their help in the preparation of this book. Thanks also to Lyle Mays, Gary Burton, Jack DeJohnette, Mike Metheny and Jay Azzolina for their time and comments. My "beyond special" thanks to my wife Aylin and my son Alex (who understands that Daddy has to disappear for hours on end to "work work work" in the studio).

INTRODUCTION: ABOUT PAT METHENY

Pat Metheny was born in Kansas City, Missouri on August 12, 1954. Starting on trumpet at the age of eight, Metheny switched to guitar at age twelve. By the age of fifteen, he was working regularly with the best jazz musicians in Kansas City.

Metheny first burst onto the international jazz scene in 1974 as a member of vibraphonist Gary Burton's group. With the release of his first album, *Bright Size Life* (1975), he reinvented the traditional "jazz guitar" sound for a new generation of players.

Pat Metheny redefined jazz with his compositions and redefined the guitar with his uniquely individual playing. He has also utilized new technology to evolve the improvisational and sonic potential of his instrument.

Since its inception, the Pat Metheny Group has been one of the most consistently successful and acclaimed groups in jazz history, earning seven Grammys for seven consecutive albums. His writing partnership with keyboardist Lyle Mays has been compared to the Lennon/McCartney and Ellington/Strayhorn partnerships.

As a "solo artist," Metheny can be seen as a Renaissance man of jazz because of the scope of his career working with artists as diverse as Steve Reich, Ornette Coleman, Herbie Hancock, Jim Hall, Milton Nascimento and David Bowie. He

Playing at the Ramada with Paul Smith, Brooks Wright, Gary Sivils (cornet), 1971

has also been instrumental in the field of guitar synthesis and has developed several new kinds of guitars such as the soprano acoustic guitar, the 42-string Pikasso guitar, Ibanez's PM-100 jazz guitar and a variety of other custom instruments.

His body of work includes compositions for solo guitar, small ensembles, electric and acoustic instruments, large orchestras, and ballet pieces, with settings ranging from modern jazz to rock to classical. (See "Discography.")

Over the years, Metheny has won countless polls as "Best Jazz Guitarist" and awards, including three Gold Records for *Still Life (Talking)*, *Letter from Home* and *Secret Story*. He has also won seventeen Grammy Awards spread out over a variety of different categories including Best Rock Instrumental, Best Contemporary Jazz Recording, Best Jazz Instrumental Solo and Best Instrumental Composition. Since 1974, Metheny has spent most of his life on tour, averaging between 120 and 200 shows a year.

THE INTERVIEWS

EARLY YEARS AND INFLUENCES

RN: The place I'd like to start is: At what point in your childhood did you think, "Music: This is it"? Where did the idea form, what was the point at which you realized that this is what you wanted to do?

PM: That's a great question. As much as I can recollect things that happened really early, I keep trying to put together what resulted in me having the life that I've ended up having. Putting together being a musician who's had incredible opportunities with the very, I'd almost have to say, straight-aheadness* of my early life—where there was no indication to

---

* When jazz musicians play music in the tradition of jazz they refer to it as "straight ahead." This would apply to jazz of the 1940s to 1960s, but would not be used to describe jazz-rock, fusion, free-jazz or Metheny's music. By the way, Metheny himself is not crazy about the description of his music as "fusion," because he (quite accurately) feels the term is far too limiting.

anybody that I was going to get much further than throwing rocks at girls in the neighborhood and not doing too well in school.

RN: That's better than doing well at school and not doing well at throwing rocks at girls.

Playing at the Lee's Summit High School assembly, 1970

PM: (*Laughs.*) Right! The key to everything would be my older brother, Mike, who was an amazing musician, is an amazing musician, at a very young age. Mike is five years older than I am and really most of the attention was rightly focused on *his* musical ability. By the time he was in junior high school (for us that's twelve, thirteen years old) he was already playing at a very high level, had an amazing, easy rapport with music and the trumpet in particular.

Performing his own compositions and arrangements with the Kansas City Philharmonic between his junior and senior year at Lee's Summit High School, Brooks Wright (drums), Dave Belove (bass), Paul Smith (piano), 1971

My early musical experiences were going to concerts
that he was either involved in or interested in. So it was all
revolving around the trumpet and trumpet consciousness in
general would certainly be the formative mechanism for my
entry into music.

I started playing the trumpet myself with Mike as my
teacher when I was about eight, him teaching me whole
notes, half notes, quarter notes, rests and that sort of thing.

With Mike Metheny and Gary Sivils, 1979

There was also a moment in the fifth grade, so I was about ten then I guess, where they bring this machine into the school and they play a very low pitch and a very high pitch and say, "Which one is higher?" Then they gradually bring the pitches together. For me it was, "Well, that first one was definitely higher than that next one." I ended up getting, even when they got to the point when it was very close together, I got a really high score. According to the guy that gave the test it was one of the higher scores, if not the highest (I can't remember exactly). That was the first indication, in terms of my own personal sense of success in music. I remember feeling like, "Wow, that's pretty cool." And also being like, "Can't everybody hear that?" When I found out there were kids who couldn't hear that, it was a little bit of a surprise to me. That would have been the first moment there was anything like, "Oh, maybe the kid's got a good ear," something like that.

RN: And your parents were musical as well.

PM: Yeah, not professional, but my dad was (and is, if he cares to be), a very good trumpet player. He's got a great sound, he can really get around the instrument well. My mom is an excellent singer with great pitch and great sound. And her dad, my grandfather on my mom's side, was a professional trumpet player his whole life. It wasn't his main job (he had a day job, too) but he would play mostly what I guess we would describe as polka music up in Wisconsin where they're from. He played a summer under John Philip Sousa in the twenties.

With Mike Metheny, 1979 (Margaret Maxwell, Osage Beach, MO)

I wondered what Pat must have been like as a kid, and who better to ask than Pat's brother, acclaimed trumpet player and composer Mike Metheny?

MIKE METHENY: Pat was very focused as a kid, especially when music became an important part of his life—probably around the age of ten. That was 1964, which was a pretty important year for pop music, the early days of the Rolling Stones and the Beatles. There was a lot happening in pop culture that had a big impact on Pat. We were also both very lucky to have a magnificent music teacher, Keith House.

It was about that time that Pat got his first guitar. He instantly disappeared into his room with his new prized possession and started to practice. His commitment really hasn't changed in the last forty years. He's still practicing!

The jazz and blues scene around Kansas City when Pat became a teenager in the 1960s was really vibrant and alive. He was in a position to go to jam sessions and do gigs with the very best jazz and blues musicians there.

Pat has always been very generous when it comes to giving me credit as an inspiration. But I've always maintained that he would have ended up becoming a great musician with or without me.

He was a very accomplished musician. All of that fed together. If you can imagine my grandfather, my mom's dad, being the father-in-law of my dad, who was a trumpet player; I remember them playing duets together. That must have been an interesting dynamic for my dad. Then when Mike came along, them playing trumpet trios together—my grandfather, my dad and my brother. So, you know, hearing and seeing all that, watching my brother practice a lot, hours every day, was just part of what it was for me. That was very formative and very important.

RN: As you know, my dad, Tony Romano, was a guitarist and singer. I'm sure you must have felt, as I did when watching my dad bringing people like Joe Venuti over to play, that you wanted to get in on the act.

PM: Yeah, and yet at the same time my trajectory would wind up being pretty different. It all kind of kicked in for me not long after the period I'm describing, where Mike was a very successful young musician more or less in the classical world. That happens to take us to right around 1963/1964—with the Beatles and everything—and the guitar suddenly appeared in the panorama of all things that a kid might be interested in as a very significant, cultural, iconic figure of . . . *something*. In terms of my own awareness it manifested in this incredible interest in the Beatles and that zone of music. It's hard to separate that initial attraction to the instrument from what that particular moment was.

That moment was one that just kind of coincidentally intersected for me with pre-pubescent angst and all that stuff that starts to kick in when you're ten or eleven years old. Ironically, as I look back on this now, that was also a very interesting moment in time for world culture. That's literally the moment that the world shifted from black and white into color TV, photographs, and everything else. I do think that for any kid there's something about becoming nine, ten, eleven, twelve years old where the world shifts from black and white into color. But for me it was a *literal* thing. Along with that comes a certain amount of natural wanting to make yourself distinct from the world around you in the form of rebellion or whatever.

The guitar became something like that for me because, the truth is, the last thing on earth my parents, my brother, anybody would have ever wanted me to do would be to play the guitar. The guitar, for whatever reason, in their consciousness represented everything not so good. It was not a band instrument; it was not a wind instrument; it was not a classical instrument. It was something that actually turns out to be correctly identified with a major shift, a major chasm in the universe at that moment—and I was attracted to it.

My present for sixth grade, if I got such and such score on such and such test, was the right to buy a guitar. Because by that time I'd lost interest in school anyway, but if I could keep my grades up, I would have the right to earn the money to buy a guitar. So I made that mark and was allowed to buy a guitar, which is a guitar that I still keep around (an ES-140 3/4, which was a Gibson, kind of miniature guitar that I got for $60 from a guy). That was the beginning of the end or the beginning of the beginning. From that point forward I literally became a different person.

What's interesting in all of this is a moment that kind of goes to your original question of "when did it all really kick in." It was when my brother brought home a record called *Four and More*, Miles Davis live. I always hear this thing about jazz being something difficult to transition into: you have to learn a lot about it, you have to study it; it's very foreign-sounding. That may be true for most people but for me, within the first five seconds of the needle touching that vinyl, my life was a different life.

All I wanted to know and all I still really want to know is what happened in those five seconds? What was that? As much as rock and roll might have offered me a window into rebellion against my parents, my brother and blah blah blah, it offered me a far wider window to become interested in jazz. Because not only could I rebel against all those people, but I could rebel against all my friends and everybody else I knew in my little town in Missouri as well. Plus, and this is maybe more important, whatever that music was, it was fascinating and inviting in ways that I had never experienced before.

RN: Did you know much about jazz culture and jazz history? Had you already been introduced to that a bit by your parents? What was your conception of what you were listening to?

PM: Yeah, I shouldn't paint a picture of my parents as being hostile to jazz. Their sense of jazz however would have been Glenn Miller, that sort of thing. The sort of popular jazz of the forties that was in fact the soundtrack of their romance together; their favorite is "Stardust" and right up and down the line in terms of popular music of that era, which was in fact triplet-based music. It wasn't country and western music; it wasn't the polka music that my grandfather played. So the music they were playing around the house was in fact a version of swing music and that kind of feeling was a feeling that I would have heard my entire life. We would go to the Kansas City Jazz Festival or to hear Clark Terry play because he was a trumpet player or even to hear Doc Severinsen, who at that time was a well-known trumpet player many years before he became this iconic, *Tonight Show*, bandleader guy. He was a trumpet star.

Kind of the same way there are guitar freaks, there are trumpet freaks. And our family was trumpet freaks, which included all styles of trumpet playing including jazz. So yes, I was dragged along to all these different kinds of concerts that involved trumpet that included jazz concerts. So in that sense I was aware of jazz but they were not really aware of it in the hardcore sense. It was more in a general sense.

Once I started really, especially with Miles, he instantly became my favorite musician and I would have to trace every early attraction to wanting to understand what jazz is to something in that Miles quintet. And I have to say there was also something about Tony Williams—the way he was playing, the sound of the ride cymbal—that had an immediate resonance to me in terms of what I was feeling in the culture. Even in Lee's Summit, Missouri, there was something about the way he was playing that in fact truly did represent a change, a major change.

I was already aware of this rock-and-roll kind of change, because of the Beatles and everything else, but there was a much deeper change going on in the world that we'd have to historically attribute to the civil rights movement. The whole sense of black power, of what was happening in the African American community in America, and in Kansas City just down the road, also figures into this in a pretty big way for me.

RN: OK, we have the influence of Miles. Then of course I remember in the old days you once said that you didn't really have formal guitar training. You actually told me a story about when you discovered Wes Montgomery. You bought a bunch of his albums and you piled them up on one side of your record player and as you memorized each album, you put it on the other side. I think you said, "When I'd memorized all of them, I went to Kansas City." Do I remember that correctly?

PM: Hearing Wes Montgomery was another massive, major change for me. There was a quality that Wes's playing had that was very much like the way Miles's music affected me. I now realize forty years down the line what some of the specific qualities that make that sound have that sort of power are.

But at the time, as a twelve-year-old kid, there was something else going that was absolutely compelling about the way Wes was playing that just made me want to listen to it again and again and again. Through that process of listening you naturally memorize things; you memorize not only what Wes was playing or what Miles was playing but what was happening underneath them and around them. Also I think that for me really understanding a few records kind of allows you a window into the whole thing.

And there was one Wes record in particular called *Smokin' at the Half Note*, which was a current record at that time, recorded in December of '65. That record became an incredible touchstone for me. But I was such a fan of Wes that all of his records, including the records that were also current at that time—which were widely dismissed critically, records that he made for Verve and then later A&M—those were favorite records for me too, for completely other reasons. They, in a much more concise way, were able to describe things that to me felt very current and very resonant and unbelievably deep.

When I think about Wes or Miles, I would also describe those two guys as being the two guys who have left a sonic residue that has pervaded all of music, not just jazz. To me there's only one other musician of recent times who I would include in that category and that's Jaco Pastorius. Their sound went way beyond jazz; it was something that became . . . you can't turn on the TV without hearing something that's reflecting that sound in popular culture. Plus, even in the most extreme nooks and crannies of the avant-garde that sound is also part of the vernacular. It's pervasive. There are very few musicians who reflect that kind of human depth in their sound. To me Wes was the guitar equivalent of Miles in that sense. Besides the process of trying to understand the mechanics of it (like why is he playing this note and not that note?) there was just this depth to it, this sound thing, which was incredibly important for me.

INFLUENCES—MILES, WES AND THE BEATLES

RN: In terms of formulating your concept it seems to me that those artists you've mentioned already—Miles, Wes and the Beatles—sum up a lot of the qualities that people would associate with Pat Metheny: with Miles, the lyricism; with Wes, the soulfulness; and with the Beatles, the catchiness, the tunefulness. I often say to my students, "All innovation is synthesis." Discuss. . . .

PM: I like the idea of looking at those three important artists as fundamental because I think in many ways that's true. I would also note however that the three qualities that you ascribe to those three guys could also be flipped around.

I mean as much as people talk about experimentation in music (and when we hear the term "experimental music," we all get quickly a picture in our mind of a certain style of playing) I would contend that the Beatles were amongst the most experimental of people that made records at the time, delivered with an unbelievably high batting average.

Wes defined his own time through a sound that could only be of his time. To me his simple playing on some of those later records where he just plays the melody of "Windy" or something like that. . . . To me (and I'm filtering this through something that we would now call a postmodern sensibility) it's much more avant-garde in a way to be able to play a solo that's eight bars long, that's that deep, than it is to play forty-five minutes of playing free. I wouldn't say that Wes was necessarily looking to do that—I think he was just doing what he did.

If we're going to talk about Miles Davis, Wes Montgomery and the Beatles, what's interesting about those three artists is that we could sit here and talk about all three of them for about fifty hours and look at it from 360 degrees, from the tiniest detail to standing in outer space and looking at a marble on earth and talk about them as well and it works on all those levels. So that's another thing that to me connects those three things, the sort of durability of what those things represent.

RN: It's interesting that you mention the tune "Windy" because there's a motif in that tune that is not dissimilar to the last phrase of "April Joy"—the feel, the phrasing.

PM: One of the mandates of the jazz form that is often overlooked is that it's a form that is quite unforgiving in its view towards nostalgia—it doesn't actually work. I don't think I've ever really heard somebody play in a style that precedes his or her time on earth. In a way it might be really, really good but it's not going to make me *not* want to hear the people that did that *first*.

I've always tried to embrace what I love and what I feel around me now. That was true early on. And in fact part of the reason that I started to write tunes was because there was a way I wanted to function as an improviser that I was not really able to do playing on a blues or playing on a jazz standard. I could play in those settings and it was fine and it's still fine; I still enjoy doing that. But there was a certain quality of something that I was not able to get to as an improviser until I started writing tunes that referenced everything that I loved. That includes a lot of qualities about having grown up out there in Missouri, a lot of qualities that are in fact related to what was happening in pop music at the time.

And there were certain things having to do with the instrument, with the guitar itself, that had not really been looked at and were fascinating and interesting and worthy to me.

Yet at the same time my earliest success as a player, around Kansas City when I was thirteen, fourteen years old, was under the auspices of sounding as close to Wes Montgomery as I could. It was a thing around town at the time. I was this little kid, I had braces on my teeth at the time, I played with my thumb and I could do a good Wes Montgomery imitation— just like there are now several thousand other people who can do it. There was a sense of acceptance and applause and "getting house" and all that stuff that came with that.

Yet, even at an early age, there was something about it that bothered me. I knew that as much as I enjoyed stepping into that guise, it wasn't really what I had to say. There's another, maybe more important part of this, which is that I loved Wes so much that I realized that in fact it's disrespectful to sound like somebody that much. Wouldn't it be better to look at Wes and say, "Wow. This guy found a way of playing that was all his own, that didn't sound like anything that had preceded it"? Why not go there, find my own thing, as a tribute to Wes rather than the overt "Here's some octaves," and so forth. So there was a point where I just said, "OK, I'm not going to do that anymore. I'm going to willfully stop ever doing that."

Then there's a period of roughness after that because that is part of what your vocabulary is, but it was a worthy moment for me to get to that place.

Playing a Gibson Crest through a Standel amp with singer Carol Comer at the Ramada Inn, Kansas City, with Paul Smith (piano), Dave Belove (bass), Brooks Wright (drums), Gary Sivils (cornet), 1971

RN: And what age was that? Because I remember you talking about the fact that you were failing school and your parents said, "You're not going to touch the guitar now until you get through school." You said that not playing the guitar helped your guitar playing enormously because you got into this "creative visualization" of your fingers playing the fretboard.

PM: Well, things happened. I look back on it now and realize that things were happening pretty quickly for me. I seriously started playing I would say when I was twelve and was starting to work gigs when I was fourteen around Kansas City, first with more what I would call amateur-type musicians (other kids my age or a little older) where we could get gigs. But pretty quickly after that, by the time I was fifteen, with some of the best players in town.

I had no interest in school anyway but by the time I started really working gigs I was barely hanging on, to the point where, for one quarter, my parents actually forbade me to play at all. I had to put the guitar in the closet and all this stuff. There was a benefit to that for me on several levels: One is that I had to really find a way to continue to practice because I think they didn't quite understand the degree to which I was already *there*. So I had to develop this way of visualizing the geography of the instrument, which I could probably space out even more by the time I got some chops* doing that, in terms of school. The other thing was that it became pretty clear to me (and I think even to them) that the train had already left the station, so to speak; there was no stopping any of this. From my dad's point of view, I think that once he saw also that I was starting to make some actual money playing gigs it became a pragmatic thing—"Well, it seems like it's working out." And then as long as I could pass whatever grade I was in, it was OK, and I kind of somehow faked my way through school.

---

* Technical instrumental ability, first used to denote the talented lips of a great trumpet player, as in, "Louis Armstrong had incredible chops!"

FLORIDA SUNSHINE

RN: At this point it's interesting to realize I've been listening to you discussing concepts you were considering at the age of fourteen! So how did an eighteen-year-old kid who had just barely scraped through high school get a scholarship to the University of Miami where you met future colleagues Jaco Pastorius, Mark Egan and Danny Gottlieb?

PM: One night I was playing a club, and this guy came in who turned out to be Dr. Bill Lee. At that time he was the dean at the University of Miami. He called me over and offered me a full scholarship. I was in shock! I went home and told my parents and it was the happiest day of their entire lives because, as far as they knew, I was gonna be on welfare soon!

My own feeling about it was: it would be a chance to get out of Kansas City. I didn't know that much about the Miami scene. There was one guy I knew there, Dan Haerle who I'd met at a band camp when I was about fourteen. He and I had stayed in touch over the years.

After literally three days of going to classes, I realized I was basically illiterate. I'd been just practicing ten hours a day and playing gigs since I was in junior high! I had faked my way through school with the help of a couple girlfriends, but there was no way I was going to be able to fake this.

Coincidentally, that same night, I heard Jaco Pastorius for the first time. I had heard about him as a musician around town. He'd even been in Kansas City playing with Wayne Cochran a few months before that, but I'd missed him. People were buzzing about him and I said, "I've gotta go check this guy out." It was everything that it could possibly have been, and more. And we instantly became very close friends and started to do things together immediately.

Dr. Lee came back to me and said, "OK, we want you to teach." The University of Miami had recently opened their doors to electric guitar as an actual instrument. And I did, at that point, have a lot of experience as a player.

GARY BURTON

PM: In the middle of that, April of 1973, there was a chance to come back to the Midwest to play a concert in Wichita—at a jazz festival I'd played before in my high school years. The guest artist was going to be Gary Burton. He was one of my favorite musicians. His band represented so many important things to me. For the chance to go and play with him, I would have walked there.

I got the chance to play a few tunes with Gary and spent a lot of time talking with him. I probably made an impression on him because I knew his tunes so well. (It would probably be like that for me—if some kid came up on stage and could play *The Way Up* in its entirety, I'd certainly notice that.)

Gary then offered me the chance to move to Boston and teach at Berklee, which is where I met you! January '74, right?

With Mick Goodrick, Gary Burton, Bob Moses, Steve Swallow, Hamburg, Germany, 1974

RN: Absolutely. What a memory! Pat, I'd just like you to talk a little bit more about Gary because we've talked before about how he was such a positive influence. To me, one of the hippest things about Gary is his ability to instantly analyze any musical situation and to tell you exactly the solution to whatever problem it is in seconds, and do it really eloquently—which is amazing.

PM: It is amazing—more amazing all the time, actually. I could never overemphasize enough the unbelievable benefits

*Grammy-winning vibraphonist Gary Burton was important
to Metheny because he "represented" exactly what
Pat would later achieve. Both men revolutionized their
instruments and both men changed the tenor of jazz,
creating groundbreaking and influential music. Throughout
his career, Burton has always supported talent and thereby
helped jazz grow as an art form. In his early years he
recorded the music of composers Michael Gibbs, Carla
Bley, Steve Swallow, Keith Jarrett and Chick Corea. He
has a tradition of taking relatively unknown musicians into
his band and promoting their careers: Larry Coryell, Steve
Swallow, Mick Goodrick, Pat Metheny, Makoto Ozone and
Julian Lage.*

*I asked Burton to relate his first impressions of Metheny
when they met in April 1973.*

GARY BURTON: Pat was eighteen years old and he walked
up to me and asked me if he could sit in. Afterwards he
asked me if I had any advice for him. I suggested that he
should move to a city where there was an active jazz scene.
He decided he would come to Boston, where he spent
quite a bit of time just following me around. I noticed right
away he was a keen observer, soaking up everything that
was going on. And I think that's one of the secrets of his
early success—he was a terrific learner!

that have come to me as a musician and as a student of music through the hours that I was able to be around Gary as a player, and also things that he would offer off the bandstand in terms of the way you analyze music, the way you look at chords, the way you fit into situations dynamically, texturally, in terms of how much activity is required in order to achieve this or that effect. And then for him to be able to go up on the bandstand and demonstrate (although it was way more than demonstration) in the most artful way—illustrate what he'd just said. The impact that had on me as a developing player was absolutely enormous.

Also I think Gary probably recognized in me that I probably was going to be a band leader at some point and was incredibly generous with letting me see the mechanics of it. He'd say, "OK, tonight we got $1000 for the whole band, I'm giving you guys fifty bucks each, but I'm keeping $600 after I pay for the gas because we're going to drive to Vermont."

He was absolutely open to me about everything he was doing. He'd also monitor my thing, in terms of tunes I was writing and all that, and would pretty much tear them apart in ways that were really quite something. He was undeniably accurate and pretty ruthless and yet at the same time not with any malintent; just kind of, "Why is it that you're looking to do this, when you could do that?" That sort of thing. And, "No, we can't play this tune because. . . ."

It was trial by fire in many ways. After three years of that I was very much ready to move on to different territory and in many ways that were in direct conflict with some of the Gary-type things, which is totally normal. I think he recognized that impulse in me from the time when he left Stan Getz; it was the same type of thing. It's the normal jazz trajectory; you play in somebody's band for a while, you take what you can from their thing and you also learn from their thing what you're not getting to do in that environment that becomes something of a goal for your own thing.

BRIGHT SIZE LIFE

To describe Metheny's first album as a leader as a "jazz trio record" is a bit like describing the Mona Lisa as a "portrait." Bob Moses had made his name as the drummer of the Gary Burton Quartet, arguably the first jazz group to utilize some of the language and rhythms of rock. Jaco Pastorius remains, many years after his death, as one of the most influential jazz musicians since the 1970s. The compositions of the leader, and the particular unique approaches of the three individuals, made this an enormously influential and evolutionary album.

RN: I'll pick a few things to discuss that represented significant direction changes or advances. Let's talk about *Bright Size Life* because it was your first solo album.

PM: Through Gary I was invited to make a record for ECM, which was an unbelievable honor and incredibly distinctive opportunity for me as a young musician. ECM at that time was the most important and interesting label in jazz and had a number of people who I would have listed as my favorite musicians at the time. It was an honor to be asked to do that.

Yet at the same time, under the guise of these many hours of discussion with Gary in terms of who I was hoping to become as a musician and where I was at, I didn't really feel ready to do it. I felt like, "Well, if I'm gonna make a record it may be the only record I ever get the chance to make so I really want to make sure it's an accurate statement about what I really believe." From the time I was extended the invitation to the time I made the record was probably a year and a half. Early on when I met Gary, not long after meeting him in Wichita, this whole idea came up. That would have been in April of '73. I didn't make the record until December of '75.

Looking at it now, it doesn't seem that long but when you're eighteen and have this incredible opportunity it seemed like an eternity to wait that long. But on the other hand the reasons for waiting, I think, ended up being worthwhile.

I knew I didn't want to make a record of standards—I could have done that, I guess, and I knew I didn't want to do a whole bunch of things. It was a process of then carving away everything and seeing what was left that I did want to do.

I can't really say too much more than what *Bright Size Life* is: a very accurate picture of where I was at that moment that in many ways reflects things that I still believe to be true. I'm happy to be able to say that. I think that many people look back on their first record and think, "Oh, man, what was I thinking?" But I still can play all those tunes and I still go, "Yup, that's kind of right, that's sort of what I feel about that."

I think that the life that record has had has been really interesting because when it first came out it got a couple of stars in *Downbeat* and kind of a snide review and sold a thousand records the first year. I remember getting a royalty statement from Australia where it had one sale—one person had bought it and I wanted to write the guy a letter but they couldn't track him down. It wasn't an enormously successful debut at the time.

But at the same time I really felt like, even though I didn't really play that good that particular day, (and of course those were one-day records), there were many things about it that I felt were new territory. And we felt so strongly about what we were doing as a trio that it's been gratifying over the years to watch the complexion of that record, the way it sort of fits into the whole music scene [which] changed pretty radically, and I often see people discussing that record in ways that are really nice. Also they're talking about many of the things that were self-evident to me at the time that maybe didn't quite fit into the community at that time in the same way.

So that association at ECM became the platform for me to leave Gary and start my own band, something I really wasn't that excited about doing. But the truth is there were very few sideman opportunities for me at that time that had the kind of opportunities musically that I was searching for. The one that I would have really liked to have done was to play in Jack DeJohnette's band—but of course he had John Abercrombie, who was one of the greatest guitar players ever. I just loved going to hear that band because it was such a great guitar spot. I had the chance to play with Stan Getz; I wish I'd done it but I didn't feel that that was right for me at that time. So in a way I had to start my own band in order to do what I wanted to do.

LYLE MAYS

RN: In the early days, I remember at one of your Boston gigs you rushed over excitedly to sit at our table telling us you had met this phenomenal musician, Lyle Mays. This turned out to be one of the most significant collaborations not only in your career, but, as it's turned out, in jazz history.

PM: I was beginning to get recognition and won a couple of polls for this, that and the other thing. I met Lyle Mays around that time. Instantly, in the same way that had happened with Jaco, within a few minutes of hearing him I felt, "Wow, we should play together." That's one of those things where you recognize a brother or kindred spirit immediately. Much like with Jaco, we hooked up really quickly and wound up playing together. I can literally remember the first notes we played together. Whatever the core of the Pat Metheny Group sound is, and has been ever since then, was there—it was there in the first four bars! As much as people may think we've worked something out, a lot of it is just the way we play together.

With Lyle Mays, Madrid, 2005

I caught up with Lyle Mays in L.A. (interrupting him during a game of pool) to ask him about meeting and working with Pat Metheny.

LYLE MAYS: It was exciting because in the first few notes I thought I heard a sensibility that I could really relate to. We have a shared aesthetic in so many areas on so many levels. There's never really been a pattern in our work. The process is continually evolving, which may be part of the secret to its longevity. It stretches from complete independent development of material that is then presented to the other person to sitting down as close as we are hammering out what a passage is, note by note.

And that became and is still a fundamental platform of what the group is. The group has always been a great spot for investigation and research. The kind of collaborative work that Lyle and I have done is often in a sort of blurry area between composition and arranging. We're taking material and processing it through our individual and collective sensibilities.

We're really kind of asking the material, "What can it be?" and "What else can it be?" There's a certain point when we're working together when I couldn't really say this is me and this is Lyle. It's us and IT. And we're interviewing IT and it's telling us things. And we rarely disagree about what IT should be. And at the same time, we have different strengths with a huge amount of overlapping. We have a lot to talk about. We've always had a lot to talk about. And we continue to have a lot to talk about.

THE PAT METHENY GROUP

The first Pat Metheny Group was a quartet with keyboardist Lyle Mays, Danny Gottlieb on drums and Mark Egan on electric fretless bass. The conception of this group was as remarkable as the Bright Size Life *album. It had to do with the particular combination of elements that very much expressed the zeitgeist of the late 1970s.*

Gottlieb's drumming had the floating cymbal work associated with the ECM sound as well as the ability to lay down an R&B groove. Egan's bass was a mixture of the Pastorius sound with the rhythmic clarity of a studio player. Even the first album established the arrangement style of the group, combining Mays's piano, synth and Autoharp with Metheny's trademark guitar sound—a Gibson 175 played through a Lexicon Prime Time.

RN: Let's talk about when you started recording with Lyle, Mark Egan and Danny Gottlieb—the first Pat Metheny Group.

PM: My second record for ECM was *Watercolors,* where Lyle and I recorded together for the first time. When that record was released it intersected with the moment when it was time for me to move on from Gary. The new Pat Metheny Group began a tour that lasted basically from 1977 to 1991. It was pretty intense on the road. We played hundreds and hundreds of concerts all over the world. Through that we developed a following that was in many ways unprecedented for a group playing the way we were playing.

The thing that's notable to me about all that is that we did it really on our own terms. We never really compromised anything. Sonically, certainly in terms of our intentions, we always played what we had to play. By doing so many gigs we gathered a following of people that really stuck with us and continues to stick with us, even all these years later. That thing of having a core constituency is a valid way of doing stuff, not just jazz but in the music world in general.

We went on to make a number of records over the years as the group under ECM's auspices. Sandwiched in between group records I was doing other types of records that were of interest to me. As the group gathered steam, the one thing I knew I didn't want to do was play on other people's records. From the moment I left Gary I made a conscious decision that I wouldn't play as a sideman on any records. If you notice,

Playing "Phase Dance," Slovenia, 1991 (tonescadej@hotmail.com)

New Chautauqua, 1979 (Joji Sawa)

from 1977 to Mike Brecker's first record in '87, anything that came out was under my own name. I sort of lightened up on that in the middle part of my career but I just wanted to focus on my own stuff. Records that came out in those in-between periods included *New Chautauqua,* which was a solo guitar record, and *80/81* which was a record that took me five or six records to get to.

I realized that the music I had played the most was music I had never documented at all because I kept thinking that each record would be the last one. I guess by that time I felt, "I guess I'll get to make a couple more." With *80/81* it seemed like a worthy project to get Mike Brecker and Dewey Redman playing together, and Charlie Haden and Jack DeJohnette had never played together. Then came *Rejoicing,* a trio with Charlie Haden and Billy Higgins, which wound up being the last record for ECM. Then it was time to move on from there.

RN: In all of the records that you've done, especially the group records, it seems that there was a certain amount of orchestration and arranging going on, even in the first group record. It's continued that way to perhaps the ultimate expression of it on *The Way Up.* You've also used that kind of very serious, composerly structure of the Pat Metheny Group as an expression of the compositions, in some ways more than the playing (not to denigrate the playing of course!), but the compositions are the thing. But then the other records, like the trio records and *80/81*, these are much more "bend over and I'll drive you home" *playing* records, "let's get out there on stage and shake our butts." Was that a conscious thing for you to say, "Okay, I'm going to have some free times and then I'm going to get structured?" Was that the contrast that you wanted?

With Mike Brecker, Dewey Redman, Charlie Haden, Jack DeJohnette, Hamburg Stadtpark, 1981 (Thomas J. Krebs Jazz Photo Agency)

PM: People often talk about my thing as something where there's a dichotomy, that there's this compositional interest that's represented in the group records, in a record like *Secret Story*, certainly in its ultimate version in *The Way Up*. And then there's the more blowing-oriented stuff, often the trio records, of which there are five or six now over the years, like *80/81* and various things I've done as a sideman.

My reaction to your question is that in many ways the impulse to combine improvisation with a lot of written material is one of the most treacherous areas in jazz. It's a very difficult thing to get just the right balance, particularly with a large ensemble where you wind up, on a human level, with a whole bunch of people sitting around counting rests. Somehow that basic human activity just adds a certain kind of energy to the whole proceedings that the audience notices and everybody senses.

In rock and roll and in popular music of the last thirty years and even before that there was always orchestration that came from an anonymous source, like background arranging. Somehow as we entered into the world of polyphonic synthesizers it was possible to invoke this broader sense of orchestration in a small group setting. That was and is a fascinating area for me.

47

The group has never been more than seven people and yet at the same time we're really writing on an orchestral scale. Some of that has to do with things we can do in the studio, where we're using the studio itself as an instrument (which to me is a very viable impulse, given that we're living in the era we're living in). Some of it is Lyle's incredible skill in this area, his unbelievable, innate sense of orchestration that involves everything he does as a player. And to a certain degree that's true with me, as a guitar player. If it means I play four notes on an acoustic guitar then switch to an electric guitar for these six notes, then have to go pick up a slide and play that, that's fine.

Those qualities of being open to orchestration are a central part of what the group thing and other things that I've done have represented and what we've offered in terms of change. It's not that we were the only ones that were doing it, either; I don't want to say that. Certainly Weather Report would be a fantastic example of exactly these same things, and it was and remains to me still fertile ground. But that is often critically characterized as less serious or more commercial or less experimental—blah blah blah. To me it's actually the contrary; to me that's more experimental, *more* difficult. In terms of being "commercial," when somebody trots that one out talking about the group, if that's true we're just stupid, because all of our tunes are twelve minutes long! If commerciality were our goal that would be the first thing we'd look at.

RN: Also, the purpose of orchestration, the purpose of arranging is to clarify the composition. I think you might agree that the prime consideration of yours is not whether this is jazz or this is pop or X, Y or Z, but whether this is the music that you intended to write. If you can clarify your composition and make it more fascinating both to you and to the listener by orchestrating it, why not do it? The Beatles certainly used orchestrations, or I should say George Martin made a tremendous contribution in clarifying the compositions with his arrangements.

PM: I totally agree.

RN: So that's all you're doing, really.

PM: I completely agree. Also, I would say that an element of orchestration is possible to do in a trio, too. It does happen at a variety of levels. I suppose what I'm saying is that it's difficult to quantify. As I look at my whole thing it's very difficult for me to come up with a stratified version of it. Yes, there's the group and then there's this other stuff. But there's way too much overlap. The idea for me all the way along has been to come up with a narrative, storytelling quality of music that hopefully adds up; once an idea starts, it gets taken to its natural conclusion. Whether that happens on a macro level or micro level, whether it's one phrase or a whole record, that's the quality I'm most attracted to. It can happen in any style or genre. That's what I'm looking for.

RN: You mentioned the storytelling quality. Some people say to talk about music in terms of "program music," for instance, telling a story, is nonsense because you can't really seriously analyze any music except in purely musical terms. That's one point of view. The other point of view says that if music doesn't represent at least an emotional story, what's the point?

PM: I think that within the whole idea of describing music in terms that are outside of the syntax of music itself you have to give a lot of leeway to different people's interpretive skills, to the whole concept of subjectivity and the poetry involved in that.

I've realized over the years that I naturally gravitate towards a very large umbrella when I say something is narrative or has a storytelling quality. If there's something that overtly lacks that storytelling quality, maybe I'll fill in my own story, and part of the story is that the guy is not doing this traditional story. To me it's a very valid method that somehow I use myself to find narrative-type qualities. When I say narrative I'm using it *myself* in a poetic sense. I'm not necessarily saying I need to hear a beginning, middle and end here. For me, Derek Bailey* is a great improviser—a very lyrical, a very narrative kind of player, not unlike Jim Hall in many, many ways. There are a lot of different ways to tell a story.

---

* Derek Bailey is a British jazz guitarist committed to "total improvisation," free of conventional conceptions of harmony, melody, rhythm, genre and form. Therefore, Metheny's use of the word "lyrical" to describe him is perhaps contrary to the way Bailey is generally perceived—and exemplifies the size of Metheny's "umbrella."

THE GEFFEN YEARS

In 1987 Metheny moved from the respected but small independent label ECM to record and film mogul David Geffen's label Geffen Records. The interesting thing about this move was that a major label would consider Metheny at all. As Metheny says below, Geffen regarded him not as a "jazz artist" but as an "artist." In our current environment of rigid radio programming and commodification of music, it is unlikely that this could happen today.

The first Pat Metheny Group albums on Geffen were Still Life (Talking) *(1987) and* Letter from Home *(1989). New elements were added to the PMG sound as Steve Rodby replaced Egan and Paul Wertico replaced Gottlieb. The focus on Latin rhythms was enhanced by the addition of Latin musicians such as Armando Marçal and Pedro Aznar.*

These albums continued a process begun on First Circle *(1984). Most significantly, the Metheny/Mays compositions*

used changing meters and became even more anthemic and
"composed." This was intensified by the even more highly textured
arrangements and the use of extreme dynamics.

RN: Let's talk a little about the move from ECM to Geffen.

PM: As the ECM era came to a close, it happened to coincide
with a high point of the amount of people that were following
the music we were making. Not only with the group but with
the other records I was making, too. Once I had made the
decision to move on from ECM, this added up to me being in
a position to come up with a very unique situation—to start
my own production company, Metheny Group Productions.
This would allow us to make our own records and then
license them to record companies.

 We actually were able to get this in operation first in
conjunction with a very popular record company at that time,
Geffen Records. Leaving ECM, it was really a very unique
situation for me because Geffen wasn't a jazz label at all. In
fact they didn't have anything remotely like jazz. At the time
the major artists that they had were . . . well, they had put
out John Lennon's last record. They had people like Nirvana,
who were just getting signed around that same time. It was a
really different environment but actually perfect because, in

Geffen publicity portrait, ca. 1993 (Jesse Frohman)

a way, they weren't thinking of us as jazz. We were just this band that had this following and they would support it. It led to a series of records that actually are the best-selling records I've had.

I realized I wanted to make the first record for Geffen a real special one. Just prior to the days that the Geffen thing got started the last record I'd made on ECM was *Rejoicing* with Charlie Haden and Billy Higgins. During that trio's extended stay here in New York we played several times at the Vanguard. Ornette Coleman came down to hear us several times and was very enthusiastic about the whole thing. He mentioned to me that he thought we should get together and play, which for me was one of the greatest thrills ever that he would even come to hear us, and then want to do something! So it occurred to me that this could be a really interesting first project for Geffen. That record became *Song X*.

Ornette and I spent a lot of time together preparing for that record and the goal both of us had was to try to make a record that was really not like any other record either one of us had ever done. That, I think, remains true and that record had a great life the first time around which was followed by an unbelievable tour. Then not long ago I was able to resurrect that record and with the CD format add a bunch of

With Charlie Haden and Billy Higgins

the tunes that didn't fit on the LP format at the time, remix and remaster the whole thing, and now it's really in great shape.

That was a great way to start the association with Geffen. It was followed by a number of the records I've made that have been the most successful in terms of the amount of copies that they've sold. The first group record there was one called *Still Life (Talking)*. It was followed not long after with the record *Letter from Home*. Those two records combined with the last group record for ECM, *First Circle*, worked for me as a sort of trilogy, a three-record set that describes a certain place that band was at that time, compositionally as well as the sound.

I was able to do other records during my time at Geffen. *Question and Answer* is a trio record with Roy Haynes and Dave Holland that was a "first encounter" kind of session. It was one of those records that you do in five hours, you play everything once or twice and that's that, very much like some of the ECM records were. Again the results were very satisfying and we wound up touring quite a bit in that configuration as well.

In the midst of all that there was a very ambitious project of mine that stands apart from everything else, which was a record called *Secret Story*. It was a culmination of everything up to that point and it involved quite a large orchestrational palette and a very ambitious kind of formal structures and writing. It was quite a project to put it together; it took an incredibly long amount of time to write the music, and recording it was a very meticulous task that took months.

That record remains for me the most successful record that I've had, even more than the group records. There have been a few records over the years that I'd almost have to describe as cult records. *Secret Story* is one and later on the duet record I did with Charlie Haden is another. There are people that are particularly into that record more than any of the others.

In 2007, there was a reissue of *Secret Story* much like the reissue of *Song X* where I added five tunes that were worked on at that same time that were never finished. [*Secret Story* was reissued by WEA/Atlantic/Nonesuch in September 2007.]

RN: To what do you attribute the success of *Secret Story*?

PM: I think that the raw emotional quality that *Secret Story* offers is something that people were always able to relate to and find some aspect of that fits in with everybody's emotional journey. Or at least everybody who has tendencies in the kinds of directions that sort of music suggests.

I also think that record has a very cinematic feel; it is almost like a movie the way it goes from beginning to end. In my opinion there's some of the best melodic stuff in terms of tunes or structures to improvise on that I've ever come up with. I still play a couple of the tunes on that record in all kinds of different settings. Even though there's quite an orchestral feeling to the nature—that music is quite expansive and big—the basic melodic material there can be played a lot of different ways, which is always a good sign whenever that's the case.

RN: In making that record you obviously had an extremely microscopically clear vision of what you wanted to do before you did it. Then it was just a question of manifesting it in the studio. Is that the case?

PM: One thing about *Secret Story* is actually I did the entire record with the Synclavier—a computer-type environment. Structurally, arrangement-wise, it exists in that form. The idea, in fact, was for that record to be a solo record, where everything you heard was me. But as we all know there's nothing like hearing a real guy investing himself or herself in some performance. As hip as everything was at that time in terms of sounds (it seemed so amazing to get that close to an orchestral depth and sensibility), I also instinctively knew that the emotional quality of the music would be so enhanced by actual stuff—real instruments. Then it was a matter of just filling in the blanks. That was a process in itself that of course takes a lot of time; in a way it takes more time to do it that way, when you've got a model that you're fitting pieces into rather than just doing it from the ground up. But the result came out good and was enhanced from the version when it was just me, by myself.

RN: Did you find when you actually recorded it that there was any deviation from what you had done? Did the players come up with anything you considered an improvement on what you had originally programmed? Or did you have such a clear vision of it that you wanted it to be pretty much exactly what you had conceived without any changes?

PM: In some ways, I wanted it exactly the way I'd conceived it. Occasionally, when people could offer their thing to it, to the point where the track would accept it, I was welcoming to it. But I would say it's pretty close to what it was. In a way that's harder too, to get someone in there and say, "No, I really want you to play exactly this rhythm." Often those kinds of rhythms that were played at one point by me are trickier than a straight-up rhythm.

RN: And of course a lot of your British fans are proud of the fact that you recorded the orchestra in London with concertmaster Gavin Wright.

PM: Well the whole orchestral side of this was enhanced by the presence of amazing London-based musicians, who for their intonation alone should be given medals from the Queen.

RN: They have been—she's a big jazz fan, and digs strings! So, how did you hook up with Nonesuch Records?

NONESUCH RECORDS

PM: After *Secret Story* there were a couple more group
records and the time with Geffen came to a close. The record
company was sold, then sold again, merged with something
else, then became a subsidiary of something else. It got to the
point where it was no longer anything more than a shell of
what it had been when I'd started at Geffen.

Mo Ostin* was still at Warner Bros. around at that time and
had been somewhat saddened that I had not continued in the
Warner world; they had been the distributor for ECM most of
the time that I had been on ECM so I had an association with
them. They really wanted to get me back, so they continued
to allow me to do this licensing thing that still goes on now.
I moved back to Warner Bros. and started there with another

---

* Ostin was a legendary executive of Warner Bros. Records. ECM had been distributed
by Warner Bros.

Warner portrait, ca. 2000 (photo by Didier Ferry/Mephisto)

group record called *Imaginary Day*. Then a couple of trio records and a solo guitar record, *One Quiet Night*, done on the baritone guitar.

The record business continued to change as it's still changing as we speak. Something very exciting emerged out of all that for me. During the early years at ECM, the guy that ran it was named Bob Hurwitz, who's just an amazing guy—great musician and a real visionary in the music world. He left ECM about the time I left to go with Geffen to become the head of Nonesuch Records, which is a label that would be very difficult to describe in relation to anything else. They do classical music, popular music and the Nonesuch Explorer series, which is probably the definitive set of recordings that describe what has happened around the world in music in terms of field recordings etcetera. They just have an incredibly high level of musicianship represented on their label.

There were several points along the way in all of this where I was very close to signing with Nonesuch just to be close to Bob. As it happens, during the time that all these reorganizations went down, Nonesuch became part of Warner Bros. In one of the last reorganizations everybody agreed, myself too, that it would be best if my stuff started coming out under the banner of Nonesuch. It's just been really fantastic to be back with Bob, one of the people that I trust the most in the music world.

THE WAY UP

After a number of eclectic releases including We Live Here
(1996), Quartet *(1997) and* Imaginary Day *(1997), new
members were added to the Pat Metheny Group for the album*
Speaking of Now *(2002). They included trumpet player Cuong
Vu, drummer Antonio Sanchez and multi-instrumentalist
Richard Bona.*

 But the most ambitious work came in 2005 with The Way
Up. *Split into four sections, only for ease of navigation with the
CD format, it is a sixty-eight-minute-long piece based on a pair of
three-note motifs. (Musicians will also note the many explorations
of the "pedal point.")*

 *New musicians who joined the group were the emotive Swiss
harmonica player Grégoire Maret and the Brazilian guitarist and
singer Nando Lauria, whose association with Metheny dates back
to 1988.*

To the best of my knowledge, this is the first time a jazz ensemble has released and toured with a sixty-eight-minute composition. Add that to the list of Metheny's innovative achievements.

PM: We were then able to do our first big production for Nonesuch, which was in fact the biggest production the group has ever done, called *The Way Up*, which was an extended piece. It took the entire length of the CD, a very involved long-form composition written by Lyle Mays and myself. It featured the group of that time. Even in these difficult conditions for record companies, it did very well and we did about a year's worth of touring around it.

Included in this whole arrangement with Nonesuch it happens that right now is when all of the Geffen stuff, starting with *Song X*, comes back into my control, the license period being over. Nonesuch is now reissuing all of those records; plus the records that I made for Warner Bros. prior to the Nonesuch move will all come out on Nonesuch. So what that means for me is that basically all of my recordings are just in two places, which is the early ECM stuff and then everything after that is all in one spot with Nonesuch. So it's pretty great for me.

BRAD MEHLDAU

RN: You've had many notable collaborators including Jaco
Pastorius, Lyle Mays, Charlie Haden, Michael Brecker
and Jack DeJohnette. The most recent has been with Brad
Mehldau.

PM: Yes, the most recent project for me [*Metheny/Mehldau*
(2006)] has been a very exciting one with pianist Brad
Mehldau, a musician I've admired since he first emerged on
the scene.

The idea of doing a project together had been hovering
around in the air between the two of us for probably ten
years or so. When I first heard Brad I literally almost had
a car accident. I'd heard about him, I knew that there was
somebody like that floating around. Josh Redman had told me
about him. But when I finally heard him playing one night

on the radio, it was everything I'd been hungering to hear from a young musician and hadn't heard—all the things about melodic development, taking ideas and really extending them, playing with that kind of great time and great imagination. And mostly having such a strong point of view of music that was rendered with such artistry. It was just what I had been hoping somebody was going to come along with. I didn't really care what instrument but the fact that it was a piano player makes it even more amazing. It's so rare to get somebody playing that instrument with such a unique, modern and innovative conception.

When I started to see interviews with Brad where he would reference me, on the one hand it was really flattering, but on the other hand I recognized right away in Brad that he was shooting for and achieving many of the ideals that I'd set for myself in those areas that I'd just described. So I could see how there would be a shared interest in certain things. We would see each other now and then and there's that typical musician thing when you close a conversation with somebody and it's like, "Yeah, we should play some time." It's like the musician version of "We should have dinner." But somehow with Brad and me, it was much more serious than that. It was like, "We should really play." "Yeah, we should play." "Yeah, right!" So this went on for a while and we're both so busy (luckily we're both able to work a lot) that I think we finally both realized that we had to get pragmatic about it and just set a date. As we all know, there's nothing like a deadline to focus one's attention.

We set a date about six months in advance of the time that we were going to go into the studio. As the date got closer we began this exchange of things via e-mail and Sibelius[*], sending each other things that we were writing and things that we were thinking about. That blossomed to the point that when we walked into the studio, between the two of us we had twenty-four pieces of music to record.

We had to decide somewhere in there what exactly we were going to do; whether it was going to be duets or quartets or what. We decided to do both. It just kind of worked out that we ended up with twelve tunes that were duet tunes and twelve tunes that were quartet tunes. I don't think either one of us ever expected that we would record all of them and that they would all work, but that's what happened. It was an incredibly productive recording period. We walked out of the studio with twenty-four tunes.

Then our friend Bob Hurwitz got involved because we didn't really know what to do with all that music. We plopped

---

[*] Sibelius is a music notation program.

it on his desk and said, "How should we do this?" We hadn't really planned on that much. Bob was the guy that came up with the idea of having two releases, the early one being mostly duet with a little bit of quartet [*Metheny/Mehldau* (2006)], the second one being mostly quartet with a little bit of duet [*Quartet* (2007)]. We've recently been touring. It's been incredibly exciting and, I think, really successful musically and an incredibly enriching experience in my life as a musician*.

RN: In Brad's liner notes he says one of the great things about playing together was that neither of you had to accommodate your playing styles at all. Interestingly enough, to me it sounds as if he has, in practice, accommodated his playing style somewhat to yours. But it's had a tremendously good effect because, as much as one can admire everything he does, when he's playing with you I think his playing is that much more accessible. I don't know why or how I can describe it in any other way. It seems to me that he has shifted his focus a little bit more towards your thing. You may say, "No, I don't think so," but it sounds like that to me.

* The tour, which the *New York Times* called a "Mutual Inspiration Society," took place in 2007 with Meldhau's regular rhythm section of Jeff Ballard on drums and Larry Grenadier on bass.

PM: Well, the thing that was interesting (having gone through the experience of playing that first day in the studio and now having a little bit of distance) is this: When you sit down and play with somebody the first time I think there's a moment when your antenna is up. You know you're going to be not only playing "Stella"* or whatever for the first time, you're going to be also handed this set of coordinates about where the person is going to plop the beat. You're going to say, "OK, he tends to hit the beat here, he tends to hit the beat there; he tends to play these types of voicings," without even registering it as that. I think we all do that. It's a little bit like that book that's out now, *Blink*†, where you get all of this information in a split second of time that then you formulate your response to.

What was interesting about that moment, the first four bars that we played together, was that both of us found out pretty quickly we could just sort of play the way we play. I think that's what Brad was implying in his liner notes. There wasn't a huge amount of adjusting that we needed to do. In my case that actually went quite a bit further maybe than Brad might think or have indicated in those notes. Usually

---

* Metheny is referring to the jazz standard "Stella by Starlight."
† Metheny is referring to the book *Blink: The Power of Thinking Without Thinking*, by Malcolm Gladwell.

with guitar and piano there's the potential for disaster pretty much front and center, voicing by voicing, chord by chord. There just wasn't any of that. At first it was almost weird to me because I started instinctively playing a lot more chords than I would normally play with piano and it all just kind of fit. It got to the point where it was more like I was playing with an organ player or something, where as a guitar player you do play a lot of chords because there's all that space between what's happening in the left-hand bass and the right-hand melodic stuff.

Some of the tracks (like if you listen to the track "A Night Away") underneath Brad's solo to me it's almost funny how much I'm comping on there and how it really works. On the tour, there's just room for that to happen and it's fine. Plus we have a way of locking up harmonically that's kind of weird. There were a bunch of those anomalies (in terms of the kind of rapport that one normally experiences as a guitar player with a piano player) that are almost inexplicable to me.

From the side of being a fan of Brad, knowing his playing pretty well and then listening to the way that he's playing in this setting, and also of course knowing my own thing to the degree that I'm able to subjectively know it, and then listening to the way that I'm playing, it's been a really good situation for both of us. We're both able to do what we do well. Also we genuinely challenge each other in good ways. And I think we both learned a lot from each other. It's been a very positive thing and amazingly fun. It's really been a blast.

THE PAT METHENY TRIO

RN: What's next for Uncle Pat?

PM: Well the last couple of years there's been an ongoing trio of myself, Christian McBride on the bass and Antonio Sanchez on drums. We've probably played 250 or 300 gigs around the world at this point and we've yet to put out a record. So in the midst of our last go-round of gigs, in the middle of the tour, we went into the studio one day in the middle of the afternoon and recorded all the tunes we'd been playing live. Then I kind of put it away and didn't really listen to it much. And then I got it all up and I'm completely blown away by what I'm hearing. It's a fantastic record.

We'd recorded a bunch of live gigs and they were really good but they sounded like live gigs. The fact that we got to do each tune three or four times meant we all zeroed in

With Antonio Sanchez and Michael Brecker, Jazz Baltica, 2003
(Rolf Kiszling)

to the real center of each tune in a way that doesn't happen
when you just play it once and go on to the next tune. It's
what studios are really good for. It's going to be a really killing
trio record. So that will come out in January 2008. [The Pat
Metheny Trio's *Day Trip* was indeed released January 2008.]

MICHAEL BRECKER'S PILGRIMAGE

Michael Brecker, arguably the most influential jazz saxophonist since John Coltrane, died January 13, 2007 of MDS (myelodysplastic syndrome) and leukemia. Coproduced by Metheny, Pilgrimage, *recorded when Brecker was very ill, was awarded Grammys for Best Jazz Instrumental Solo and Best Jazz Instrumental Album.*

In an interview I did with Brecker in London for the BBC in 2006, Brecker said, "I can't say enough about Pat. I don't have words to describe what I feel about his playing."

PM: Another big project for me this year was the release of Mike Brecker's last record, which I was very involved in. Mike was one of my dearest friends and one of my major musical collaborators. In the midst of his incredible battle he made what is to me not only his best record, but one of the best records anybody's made, called *Pilgrimage*. That record will forever have a special place for all of us that were involved in playing it. It's a pretty amazing testament to Mike's power as a human being but also just his amazing musicianship.

JOHN PATITUCCI: Like many musicians of my generation, when Pat's records started to come out, they had a big effect on me. I've known his music pretty intimately. Finally over the last several years we got the chance to hang out and do a little playing. Most recently, the big thing we did together that will probably be etched upon our souls for the rest of our lives is that we both participated in Michael Brecker's final recording.

Mike and I had been friends for over twenty years and Pat's known him even longer than I have. That was an amazing experience—the vibe in the studio, how Michael was playing so strong, Pat was the consummate producer, artist and musician—great guitarist, great sound and great everything—whatever you need, it's there!

During the rehearsals, Mike was playing so great that Pat was saying, "C'mon, Mike! You're not really sick, are you?" In fact Mike was doing so well that Pat was saying, "You're playing so strong on this record! Why don't we do a few gigs

It's compositionally one of the most cohesive and deep sets
of tunes I've ever run across some guy coming up with for a
record date. He put together just the right band for it and after
not playing for a year and a half somehow played absolutely
at Mike Brecker level, which even sitting a few feet away from

in New York?" And Mike was really into the idea, because he
was really superhuman on this thing! We were really caught
up in the idea. The tunes were amazing. Herbie and Brad
Mehldau played piano, DeJohnette played drums.

It was very moving for all of us. I loved Mike for a lot of
reasons. The reason I live in this town is because Mike lived
here and told me about it. He and his family came to the
hospital when both my daughters were born. As a kid I used
to transcribe his solos. He was a big influence on my playing
in terms of helping me find my own voice.

Pat's legato and liquid approach to melody also had
a big effect on my phrasing. If I had to use a word to
describe Pat's music it might be "heartland" because that's
where he's from. It reminds me of Copland, Americana
in the idealistic sense combined with Pat's incredible
sophistication. It's got all the natural beauty and earthiness
of the Midwest combined with a profound understanding of
the jazz canon and vocabulary.

him while he was doing it I have no idea how he did it. So that's an amazing part of what my recent life as a musician has been, being involved in everything around Mike.

COMMUNICATION

Metheny's long hair, jeans and striped T-shirts may have made him more accessible as an artist to teens of the 1970s, who saw him as one of their generation. But it was his music, an irresistibly personal combination of jazz, rock, country and blues with a Beatle-ish melodicism, that communicated universally to all generations.

RN: Why has communication been so important to you?

PM: Anybody who aspires to do anything at a high level is somehow trying to reconcile their existence with something that goes beyond what they can understand. Music itself is a very interesting commodity in the spectrum of the things that surround our time on earth. I mean, you can't smell it, you can't taste it and you can't see it. But when music is doing what it's supposed to do, it's interesting how everybody can feel it. And it's interesting to consider the power that it has.

At the same time, a guy who becomes the world's greatest architect is also able to imagine something that doesn't exist and bring it to life. For that matter, a guy who's an excellent car mechanic is able to see a problem and somehow reconcile his place on earth at that moment with that particular issue and achieve a certain resolution.

And the way that all this overlaps with existential issues of religion and the "big questions" that we all wrestle with is inseparable. Yet at the same time I've learned so much—not only from the process of being a musician, but from music itself. And I have to say there's a power and appeal to a genuine understanding of music that sets it apart. And I recognized that very early on.

As far as the impulse to share that, whatever my nature is—if I notice something cool—I want to tell other people about it. Whatever it is, a new song or something going on in the world, I want other people to know about it. I also want to see what other people think about it. So I think that's all just kinda built in for many of us to want to compare notes and share the things we've found to be true or of interest.

GARY BURTON: Pat is one of the most successful jazz musicians in history. He has very large audiences and a great fan base. For one thing, he is a very melodic player, and I think that's a key element for any successful jazz musician. But I think above all else he has a terrific natural charisma—he really communicates to the audience extremely well. I've sometimes watched him play for large audiences of thousands of people and I can really feel his personality emanating right off the stage into the audience. He understands them very well, but that doesn't mean he plays down to them—far from it. He in fact is saying to them, "I have something important that you need to hear. Pay attention and this is going to really be something for you." That message comes across and people pay attention.

DEDICATION/OBSESSION

RN: To achieve excellence requires dedication. To achieve excellence and have success requires even more dedication. To achieve excellence and success on your level and be a significant innovator requires a mind-boggling level of dedication bordering on obsession. Discuss!

PM: (*Laughs.*) The bass player in my band for the last twenty-plus years has been a fantastic musician, Steve Rodby. He's a close friend and a very important colleague in so many ways, both on and off the bandstand. He was asked about me in an interview, and the term that he used which I thought was both accurate and kind of funny was, "compulsively productive." That kinda does hit it on the head.

And, yes, there is an overlap between dedication and the point where I understand why my parents were very worried about me when I was thirteen years old, practicing ten or twelve hours a day. If one of my kids were to do that with something I didn't completely understand, I would probably be really worried, too.

People are quick to recognize the benefit that comes from dedication, and are willing to let a lot of other things slide—whatever behavior that might be wrapped up with this. That's why you see so many wacky kinds of musicians floating around with all sorts of odd personality quirks, yet are allowed those quirks by their friends and family. The quirks in themselves have become a lifestyle for lots of people who really don't have that much going on as musicians! That's an interesting post–Beat Generation phenomenon. We have people now who are all about the pose with none of the actual content.

But the culture that surrounds music has never been that much of an interest to me. It's been more about the result. So in that sense, as much as I would acknowledge the "compulsive/productive" piece of what make me do what I want to do, I would be pretty happy to do it if it were just me in a room by myself. Communicating it and sharing it with people is a happy by-product of the result.

The truth is, when it comes time to play, I'm playing what I know to be true. Because I think the moment you start guessing—the moment you see that guy in the third row who's got his arms folded and seems to be really bored with the whole proceedings—the moment you read a review that was less than complimentary—that's when you're in big trouble if you let it encroach even the tiniest bit into your "zone." Because the only thing you know is what you love— what it is to *you.*

So I'm happy to offer whatever I've found through the research, but I would also be pretty happy to move to the middle of nowhere and just do it. I think the result would be very similar in terms of the notes—the representation might be different.

ADVICE

RN: We talked about obsession, drive, fire, and dedication. Whatever you had of those elements gave you no choice but to excel. What advice would you give to somebody who wants to shift his or her dedication into overdrive?

PM: When I meet a young musician who seems promising, one of the most essential questions I pose, and it's very difficult for most people to answer, is a simple one: "What do you want to do?" It's amazing how many people don't have a picture of what they want to do in their mind.

That was a question I was extremely aware of very early on. I had a pretty good picture in my mind, not just of what I wanted to do. I could see it. I could see the band, I could see the setup on the bandstand, I could hear what it was gonna sound like, I could imagine the kinds of players in an idealized version. That's a big component in kicking things into that next stage of development. Being able to really have a goal—a tangible specific sense that's also realistic of your future. Maybe it's a year from now, or two years from now. Maybe it's tomorrow. Picture something that you're immediately able to start working on. It's NOT: "Well, if I can get this piece of gear" or "If I can play with that guy" or "If I can move to this city" or "If I can get a record deal." It's amazing how many people will wait years for one of those things to come into place when they could have been instantly working on whatever they really need to be doing. Usually it's just between where you're at and where you want to be as a musician.

RN: Your brain, like any talented person's brain, has a wide frame of reference. But you also have the ability to connect those things you know about in a unique way. What advice would you give people who want to develop that connectivity?

PM: Well, the second question I would pose to somebody is "What do you love? What really does it for you? I know you're supposed to like Clifford Brown, but when you hear those records do you really love them? Or is the truth that you really get knocked out when you hear Radiohead?"

My feeling is, what you love is an incredibly accurate compass that lives inside of you, telling you what you should be doing. Of course we all need to expand our horizons constantly. We've all had the experience of hearing something and saying, "Oh my God! I never knew that even existed! That's the greatest thing I ever heard!"

But there's a second part to that: At that moment you thought it was the greatest thing you ever heard. Are you going to listen to it again and again and again the same way

With Herbie Hancock, Dave Holland, Jack DeJohnette, Europe, 1981

I did when I first heard Clifford Brown? Being compelled to want to listen to something over and over again is an amazingly useful thing to pay attention to.

If it's something that you love that much, my feeling is that it's something I want to learn to play. I want to know how that works. How are they doing that? My first impulse when I heard Herbie and Tony and Miles playing "There Is No Greater Love" was that it sounded great to me. Then I thought, "OK, it says 'There Is No Greater Love.' What is that, a song?" I'll never forget when I was about a year older, around thirteen, finally understanding that they were playing a form that was recurring. It was the greatest revelation I'd ever had. I couldn't stop smiling for a week. I had gotten into the code of it!

And now, all these years later, if I hear that same track, I'll hear a million things I never heard before. My understanding, in terms of the dialect that's being spoken, is light-years more evolved than it was then. But I'm still compelled to want to hear that.

That's the key right there: to follow that compass.

SELF-CRITICISM

RN: I've worked with a lot of great artists functioning at a very high level. And I've found most of them to be self-critical to an extent that mere mortals might consider a little "over the top." Having also worked with you, I feel you might be a good person to ask about this.

PM: On the panorama of critical people—with one being someone who's not critical and ten being someone who's very critical—I would be eight, easily, if not more.

I rarely hear something I'm playing on that I'm happy with. So what constitutes a mistake or being acceptable or not is a real slippery slope for me to begin to quantify.

If I'm doing a record date and I get two takes, I'll say, "Let me hear both of them'" and then, "The second one is a little bit better than the first one."

Metheny in checks—no stripes

But then there's another thing: I'm gonna do a tour that's gonna last a year and I'm gonna play maybe a couple of the same tunes every night. Within that frame of mind, the possibility of self-criticism becomes infinitely more expansive, to the point where it becomes "I should be playing a flat-nine on that chord rather than a natural-nine." Then it becomes, "HOW do I play that flat-nine?" Then it becomes, "What dynamic level do I play that flat-nine?" Then it becomes, "What side of the pick do I use to play that flat-nine?" Etcetera.

And each night when that moment comes up, those questions and that sense of what makes something correct and not correct come into play. At that point, we're crossing into the territory we discussed before and is probably best described as "mental illness." (*Laughs.*)

PRESSURE AND PREPARATION

RN: Pat Metheny and pressure. Discuss.

PM: Given the music that I play and the type of person I appear to be, I would think that most people don't think about my world as one with a lot of pressure surrounding it. But every night I'm playing for people who mostly took a shower before the gig, parked their car and had to buy their ticket. And I'm lucky to be able to play with some of the best musicians on the planet. It's one thing to make one record and have it be pretty good. But to make record after record and make them all at a certain level . . . and actually that's not enough. It has to go beyond each time.

It does add up to a certain kind of lifestyle that I've had to adjust to. Whether I could say that I thrive on it or not, time will tell. The fact that I've been able to hang with it for so long, and I'm still standing, is probably something on the positive side.

I can't say that I enjoy a certain kind of pressure. But I find I can alleviate it by preparation. For that reason, before an important playing situation, if I can I try to memorize the music. That may take days, but it's worth the time that takes to alleviate the kind of pressure that is not the good kind of pressure. If I'm really comfortable with the music, then I can get to the more interesting kind of pressure—the ability to invoke many of the conceptual kinds of things you and I have been talking about—elements that are more at the heart of whatever my thing is—rather than worry about something like, "Is this a C minor or a C seventh?"

And there are many subgroups of that preparation. There's a whole ritual of what I need to do before the concert each night, a set of things I've found to be useful to allow me to get to the point where the first note of the concert is a moment where I'm really ready to address music with everything that involves. Which includes a certain amount of pressure in a way that I think is probably good. It's a little bit like the good cholesterol and the bad cholesterol! (*Laughs.*)

MARATHON GIGGING

RN: Speaking of pressure, some people might also consider your idea of gigging to be rather daunting—sometimes averaging 200 gigs a year with a typical concert lasting three hours.

PM: I see any chance to play as a privilege, and as the years go on I feel that even more so. It's such an incredible opportunity to be on earth in my favorite possible way. To be able to take a look at music in the best possible environment, that's what playing with great musicians is. I always feel kind of like each concert; that could be IT! And that's kind of a cliché that certain musicians play as if every gig is the last gig. But in my case, that's actually true. It doesn't matter to me if there are only five people there.

If I'm going to play "Mary Had a Little Lamb" for my kid's class, accompanying them on guitar (which I do), I still have

On Stage (Kevin Morley)

to warm up for like two hours! (*Laughs.*) And again, we're crossing into the mental illness thing.

In the context of my group, which is where the most extended concerts tend to happen, first of all we're talking about a band that has a thirty-year-plus history with an incredibly big book—a bunch of music that is really worth playing. Even after all this time, it's really fun and exciting music to grab a hold of. And as the years go by, the value that's intrinsic to some of those pieces becomes even clearer to me in a sort of "me-to-me" sense. I really do believe that the bridge to "First Circle" is really cool. Yes, that is something worth doing. So when it's time to put together the set list, it's often five or six hours long, not three!

RN: OK. But you don't even stop in the middle for milk and cookies!

PM: I actually think if we took a break, it wouldn't work. When it really gets good, it's one long tune. In fact, I could say that my whole career has been one long tune. From the first gigs I played up 'til now, it's really been one long set. There is a consistency and continuity there that makes this all one continuous process.

ART AND REALITY—
JAZZ AND ENTERTAINMENT

RN: Well, since we're having so much fun with all this conceptual stuff, let me throw caution to the winds and throw this at you: The German philosopher Friedrich Wilhelm Nietzsche said, "We have Art so that we shall not die of Reality." Discuss!

PM: Yeah, that Nietzsche guy. (*Laughs.*)

One thing about jazz is the way that it demands that a person offers a certain kind of individuality to each moment. Jazz guys are asked to report on their time on earth in a way that's best served by a certain kind of immediacy—the kind of thing that improvisation is perfectly suited to do.

In that sense I would say that it's more of a hyper-reality. It's not a substitute for reality. It only becomes a substitute for reality when jazz becomes nostalgic. Because I don't think it's possible to recreate a previous era in jazz. Jazz actively resists that.

For that matter, I don't think an individual musician can recreate something they did before. If I wanted to redo my own record from thirty years ago *Bright Size Life*, I couldn't do it.

In that sense, jazz is separate from entertainment and is closer to the qualities that have been associated with classical music. However, I don't think jazz works as classical music, as much as people try. We can find great notes written on a page, like Duke Ellington. Yet hearing Duke's amazingly great notes played out of the context of his existence and his spirit, as much as it might have a certain entertainment value, it always seems to ring hollow. It doesn't seem to have the other value jazz demands from people to express something not only about who they are, but the time that they're living in.

RN: Absolutely, but bringing us back to the relationship between Art and Reality, you take your listeners somewhere else, out of our world where there's violence, killing, torture, greed and politics. Your listeners perceive that place your music takes them as more spiritually aware, more true to the way existence *should* be than the way it is. Surely you can only do that because when you conceive of the music, it's doing the same thing for you.

PM: There's a certain craving, a certain desire that we all have for transcendence. This is often found in the way that people look for religion or attempt to find some spiritual center to how they conduct their activities. That's worthy of note and I have my own journey in that area.

I would agree that my attraction to music is largely about trying to find some meaning in the midst of everything that I can then filter through my own experiences. Hopefully it comes out sounding like something that somebody might want to hear.

Whenever it comes up that people are looking for an intersection between music and spirituality, the only thing I can say is: Any kind of humility you can bring to the bandstand, or that you can face music with, is usually valuable in terms of the result in sound.

Whenever a musician seems to be really sure of what's going to happen, there can be an early payoff to that, but it seems to have diminishing returns. Whenever a musician can invoke this sense of wonder and awe about what music is, that seems to offer a much longer path towards something we're all looking for—which is something that continues on. My connection to music is one that follows that. I try to remain in service to music rather than the other way around.

THE ABILITY TO IDENTIFY

RN: Every action is significant. Choosing a note is an action.

PM: Oh, I completely agree with that one.

Sometimes finding the right first note is all you need. Often in the process of writing music, the first micro bit of information literally contains everything you need. One of my favorite ways of describing this is: Music is everywhere around us. Our skill level is really the ability to identify more than the ability to create. If you can use your skill as a tool that can extract something without breaking it, you're given a window into a set of possibilities that offers you infinite possibilities—if you have the ability to identify them. And that ability comes with practicing, study, general insight into existence and life, and all the other things necessary to become a good musician that have nothing to do with music. All of that seems to increase the precision by which you're able to extract things from this infinity of music that surrounds us at all times.

RN: The groove unifies the artist with the listener. You have constructed some quite unusual, rather sophisticated grooves using multiple meters. Is your aim to unify on a more sophisticated level than, for instance, "Let's go out and have a burger"?

PM: (*Laughs.*) The only listener I know anything about is myself. I'm constantly amazed and mostly puzzled by how other people perceive music. Sometimes it's all about clothes and haircuts and fashion and cultural divisions that are being projected under the auspices of music. I have no idea what they're talking about.

For that matter, when people say, "This is heavy metal, this is emo, this is punk, this is pop, this is rock, this is jazz," mostly, I don't know what they're talking about. In terms of the context that I'm looking at music in, none of this matters at all. I have absolutely no sense of how anybody else perceives anything. And I hate to say it: that includes the majority of people who would come to a gig of mine.

I just try to play for the listener inside me. And yes, in answer to your question, that listener does want to hear things he has not heard before—an odd time signature, a certain kind of harmony, whatever. The fan that I am of music has an incredible hunger for hearing new things. When I'm writing

With Steve Swallow and John Scofield, Perugia, Italy, 1994 (Carlo Pieroni Tolentino)

something I'm not usually aware that it's in any particular time signature or key. I think more in terms of what existed in that first little burst of the idea that put me in that territory to start with, and then try to follow it—let it be whatever it's going to be.

I will add though that I'm very sensitive and aware of what the strengths are of the people I'm playing with. To a large degree, I'm ordering up things that are going to suit those people. If I do a tour playing with Roy Haynes, that offers different opportunities than if I'm doing a tour with the Group, and vice versa. I've always loved something that Steve Swallow used to describe when it's time to write tunes. It's like ordering a burger at a deli: As you're walking to the deli you think about wanting a burger and what you'd like to have on it and then you place your order. To a certain degree, there's an act of faith there that at a certain point, you're gonna get the burger!

With a tune it's sort of like that: I need an up-tempo tune that's going to be on that tour with Roy that's coming up. I didn't ask for a grilled cheese sandwich with lettuce and tomato, I asked for a burger with pickles. I placed my order. In the case of a tune, it may take a week or a month or a year, but what's funny is: that tune tends to show up.

THE GUITAR: METHENY'S MUSICAL CREATIVITY APPLIED TO THE GUITAR

Pat Metheny has explored, expanded and revolutionized the guitar. Most guitarists would have been satisfied to come up with a unique, signature sound and use that for their whole career. Not Pat!

After coming up with a very personal sound with his Gibson ES175 processed through a Lexicon Prime Time with multiple amplifiers, he worked with a variety of other guitars. On the song "Letter from Home," he played a soprano mini-guitar developed with a little help from Ibanez. He used acoustic and electric six- and twelve-string guitars in unusual tunings. He developed the Roland Guitar Synthesizer and the Synclavier Guitar ("Are You Going With Me," "Daulton Lee"). He used a fretless nylon-string guitar on "Imaginary Day" and acoustic ("Tears of Rain") and electric Sitar-Guitars ("Last Train Home"). He developed a whole

Amsterdam, 1991 (Rob Becker/Beeldverhaal Amsterdam)

range of acoustic guitars including the 42-string Pikasso guitar. He also created the PM100 for Ibanez, a new body shape for an electric jazz guitar.

As respected jazz guitarist Jay Azzolina told me, "He made the guitar a new instrument in terms of his unique sound and

Playing the Pikasso guitar

Playing the classical guitar

phrasing. Even if we ignore all the new instruments he introduced, it was a reinvented instrument because of the way he played the guitar."

If his relationship with his instrument were a novel it would be both a love story and an adventure, with liberal elements of mystery and science fiction. I think you'll also find it a "page turner" in this book!

To those readers who are amazed by Metheny's impressive guitar technique, his incredible sense of time, his swing, his groove and his taste, his own view of the guitar may be surprising. . . .

THE "INSTRUMENT" OF THE IDEA

RN: I think it's significant that we call something we play notes with a musical "instrument." The word "instrument" is significant. It is no more than an instrument we use to express ourselves, like we use a spoon to drink soup or a doctor uses a scalpel to perform an operation. Many people get hung up concentrating on the instrument rather than the expression, like concentrating on the shiny silver spoon rather than the delicious soup.

PM: Yeah, that's a good one—I'll have to use that!

I do think that there are musicians who are in love with their instrument to an extreme degree. I was never that into the guitar. I liked the guitar. I was attracted to it, like a billion other kids, probably because of the Beatles. In 1965, what the guitar represented was certainly comin' right up Sixth Avenue towards me as an eleven-year-old kid. But it was never like, "Wow! It's the guitar!" It was more about the music with the guitar as a component of that. I wanted to understand all of it, not just the guitar part.

And in a way, the guitar remains an oddball in jazz. It has some difficulties as an improvisational instrument because of its very limited dynamic range, dynamics being such an important part of expression. On the other hand, I feel very proud to often be included in a small group of guys who have worked really hard over the last thirty years to bring the guitar into the improvisational panorama of what's possible by offering some stuff that you can't get any other way.

Whether I play the piano or the trumpet or the guitar, I'm going to play the same thing. I'll play it better on the guitar because I can play it better. But the idea starts for me before the instrument, because it's not the guitar that I'm playing— it's the idea.

What I always try to explain to people is that many players are really involved in playing their instrument and what I find is that those are the players that you tend to enjoy for a little while. And maybe by the second tune you enjoy them a little bit less and then the third tune, a little bit less. Then by the fourth tune you're either asleep or out of there because it's mostly about them playing an instrument. It's certainly that way with me in a much more condensed form. I very quickly get a sense of somebody's connection to either instrument or idea as his or her entry point.

For me, the idea is completely the dominant factor, because the truth is I don't really play the instrument that well, relative to several hundred thousand other people. The playing of the instrument is almost incidental because the idea should dominate and should win. So, say I have an idea that if I played it on the piano it would be this:

EXAMPLE 1. *Metheny plays three notes on the piano.*

... which is a very simple idea. Yet at the same time that idea, translated through a touch, a way of hearing sound and a general conception of music, could communicate my personality.

I don't know if those three notes on a record would carry my total identity, but it would come pretty close, especially if I played it on the guitar. It's the sound, the touch, the dynamics, the nature of the instrument all working together to create whatever thing exists that's in my part of the world. But that idea is strong enough that there are a million things I could do.

EXAMPLE 2. *Metheny uses those three notes on the guitar as the basis for an improvisation. (© Pat Metheny Music)*

All of that other stuff—personality, the qualities of what a good improviser can bring to the way it connects with the bass and the drums and the room and the audience and all that—becomes the real meat of what makes the music sound like music. The idea is just the envelope for all that stuff to happen, with the instrument being fifth or sixth or seventh or eighth on the priority level.

Metheny with a few of his instruments (photo by Latifa)

Now for somebody who's playing the instrument from an *instrument* standpoint, this whole issue of ideas often is not even in the top ten. It's more like the ideas are just an envelope for them to do this, that or the other thing. What I notice with a lot of jazz is that it lacks ideas. It's more about other things.

THE SOUND

RN: I remember back in the Berklee days, you rushed up to me in the hall saying you'd found this great thing, the Lexicon Prime Time. It allowed you to get a sound that was not a rock sound or a jazz sound, but something new—a sound with both electric and acoustic qualities.

Most people who'd invented a new guitar sound, as you did at the beginning of your career, a very recognizable Pat Metheny sound, would have been very happy with that for the rest of their lives, but not you. Oh no. You had to go and invent a bunch of guitar sounds and use a lot of very interesting, very recognizable new guitar-type things.

PM: The whole issue of sound was so intensely important to me early on, for a variety of reasons, many of which we've already covered.

I had an occasion one time (it was a tour in the Soviet Union in 1987) where I was invited to attend a jam session the night before one of our concerts as we arrived in a new town. I really didn't feel like it because I wasn't feeling good and all the kind of things that happen when you're on the road. It was a difficult travel day and a big concert the next day. But it was indicated to me, "No, you should really go. You kind of have to go to this."

So I went to this place. It really wasn't a jam session; there were about five thousand people there. It was in a gymnasium; there were several local bands. This was in Kiev. They're playing, and me and the other guys I'd managed to drag along with me from the band were expected to get up and play. There were TV cameras everywhere. It was one of those things you really could not say "no" to.

So I had to get up there and play with this band, playing on a Russian guitar through a Polish amp. It was just completely the most foreign thing I have ever experienced in terms of stuff. And it was broadcast on TV. I went home to the hotel and it was on, in an hour delay. It was a big deal. That in itself is pretty amazing.

But as I was listening to this I realized it sounded exactly like me. In fact it occurred to me, "Why am I bringing all this gear around with me?" It was like in one half-second all of my theories about digital delays* and gear and amps around the stage (which had been almost self-defining in so many ways for me in terms of my relationship to getting a sound and an identity), I realized that I had been missing the forest for the trees, as the saying goes.

Those are components in defining a sound, and it doesn't hurt to have all that stuff—but it's totally a conceptual issue that happens in your sensibility as a musician that doesn't even have that much to do with the instrument. From that point forward I have to admit, I felt a lot *freer*. I realized it's not really what I thought. It's sort of this thing that is quite separate from any of the mechanics.

By that time I was already interested in what the guitar could be, what we could offer our fellow musicians that guitarists up to that point had maybe overlooked. The guitar is a unique instrument in the panorama of instruments. You say "guitar"—every single person that hears that has a completely

---

* A device for processing sound. It records or "samples" the signal and plays it back delayed by a programmable amount of time. When played back with the original signal, various effects are possible from the illusion of double-tracking to chorus-type effects to different ambiences. Metheny was probably the first guitarist to use this as a signature sound when he discovered the Lexicon Prime Time. This allowed him to create a new sound comprised of the original guitar signal plus that signal delayed by approximately six milliseconds, plus a longer delay on one side of the stereo and an even longer delay on the other side. The delays are carefully mixed together in the appropriate proportions to give Metheny an electric guitar sound with acoustical qualities. Acoustical, because if you play an instrument in a large hall (or if you live near a cave or a fjord), you will hear reflections of the original signal delayed in a similar way, reaching your ear at different times.

different idea of what you're even talking about. For some people it's an amplified acoustic guitar, played by a guy in a chamber music environment; to some people it's the guy in Megadeth with sixteen Marshalls playing Wembley Stadium. It's all guitar.

For me and a number of my contemporaries (Bill Frisell comes to mind, John Scofield definitely comes to mind and a number of others) we've really been involved in this research to find things we can offer the music, our fellow players, that are valid and interesting. We hopefully offer some qualities that are usable and help move the stories along.

So seeing I wasn't attached to any piece of hardware, that threw open a world of potential that I then embraced even more fully. Doing things with guitars in terms of tuning, processing, not processing, acoustic, electric, mixing the two, with even more intensity and trying to explore that stuff.

NOTE WORTHY

RN: I'd like you to pick up your nice guitar again and talk about and demonstrate your concept of motivic development.

PM: (*Picking up his guitar.*) This is a hard one. . . .

RN: No, this is the Ibanez PM100. . . .

PM: (*Laughs.*) OK, let's just do D minor to B flat. We have a motif, so I'll just kind of work that. [Metheny plays here, accompanied by bassist Janek Gwizdala, who assisted me in this interview.]

Example 3. *Metheny's motif* (© *Pat Metheny Music*)

RN: Using this in terms of some of your compositions, as we've talked about before, composition is just slow improvising. So a lot of your early tunes were based on interesting uses of an interval, like the seventh interval in "Unity Village" and the fifth interval in "Bright Size Life." Will you demonstrate how just one interval can be used as a goldmine of melodic material for an improviser?

PM: "Bright Size Life" is a good example because it represents the development of an idea that's based around a perfect fifth, which is one of the most appealing motivic universes to explore for me. You can just keep soloing in the style of the melody and it sounds fine. So, I'll reference the melody a little bit, then keep going with the idea of fifths rather than playing the whole tune. Let's play the first eight notes, then we'll just be blowing.

EXAMPLE 4. *Metheny's motivic approach to "Bright Size Life"*
(© *Pat Metheny Music*)

The bridge has [*plays motif*] that being a development
within itself of this major seventh idea but implied over
dominant seventh chords, which is kind of cool. And then that
inverts with another version of that later on. So we'll play that
and then just play on the form. . . .

EXAMPLE 5. *Metheny's bridge and solo on "Bright Size Life"*

(© Pat Metheny Music)

TASTE VS. "CHOPS"

RN: How does a musician who has a relatively high degree of technical virtuosity, and the ability to play just about anything, develop the taste *not to?*

PM: That's a very good question that really should be asked more often. I would actually say it's a problem for most musicians that do achieve a certain level of fluency. I wouldn't even relegate it to "chops" or velocity or any of those things.

How can a musician who has that particular set of tools understand that if you're going to fix the roof you don't use the same tools you would use to put in a garbage disposal in your sink? You need different tools for those. People often get so excited by the fact that they can fix their roof that they don't really work on the interior that much.

In fact, there's a degree of finesse and subtlety involved in the minor details of a good improvisation or story, which needs to happen in order to be told in the most interesting way. You wind up with people who have these good global structures without too much going on underneath. I was really lucky again to have been around lots of really good musicians, who had incredible fluency, incredible skills and were very mature about how they deployed those skills. Gary Burton comes to mind as a great example of this. I would say the same about Steve Swallow. Mick Goodrick is a good example of that. Those were very formative figures for me to be around at age eighteen, nineteen years old. To see them have all of this "fire power" available and willfully not use it is impressive.

In recent times I'd have to include Brad Mehldau in that group. He has an amazing patience to just kind of wait out ideas and not do what he can do easily—almost ever! It's amazing how he is really willing for long periods of time to go by without any overt activity and then suddenly there's this whole other thing going on which makes it have even more weight and meaning.

RN: Here's another quotation for you. (I know you love these!) Quentin Crisp said, "To have style is to be yourself but on purpose."

PM: Well, one of my favorite quotes that has so much resonance for me I continue its place on the top of the charts is: "The things that are the most personal ultimately become the most universal." Which I think fits very well with what you just said. And I really believe that's true, that the more deeply you can understand the things that you care about and that you love in music, the closer you'll be to being able to be an effective ally of music to the people who might be out there listening to you.

MELODY

RN: What's the difference between "a melody" and "not a melody"? What makes one group of notes a melody and one group of notes not really a melody?

PM: Well, melody in general is the most impossible aspect of music to nail down. I often see people and I can tell they think they're playing "melodically." And it is in that, if you were to break it down, it is melodic—but it doesn't really work as melody.

The thing is with chords, if you play these sets of tones under these conditions, there's no denying it—that's a B♭7(♯11)—that's what it is; there's no discussion necessary. There are attempts to quantify melody under the guise of jazz education or the general way that melody is described in classical-oriented studies. For example, certain kinds of intervals invoke lyricism; certain kinds of intervals invoke romance, etc. And that's all well and good and you can do those kinds of things.

But when you hear, for instance, Lester Young or Stan Getz or (at a much higher speed level) Clifford Brown, there's a genuine melodic quality at work there—in a poetic-melodic sense—that goes way beyond anything you can quantify. Gary Burton would also be a good example, as would Bill Evans and Jim Hall.

As much as you try to break down what a melody is, it ultimately becomes a poetic definition. You can't really break it down. And it's also the rarest thing today; you rarely hear somebody who's a really good melodic improviser. It's possible to become a pretty good abstract improviser knowing this, that and the other thing. And it's possible to become a pretty good bebop improviser. But for somebody to really devote a certain amount of their efforts as a musician or their practice time to becoming a good melodic player, what do you even tell them to practice? What is it exactly? You can't really break it down. It's something that goes beyond the nuts and bolts of any discussions that we can have about things.

Yet at the same time, when I say "melodic" myself, I'm going to have to invoke a certain amount of artistic license. I would make a pretty strong case that Jack DeJohnette drum solos are melodic, as are those of Paul Motian. But we're not talking about pitches there; we're talking about a sense of unfolding and a way of describing time and doing it with this sensibility that could only be described as "melodic." Max Roach would be another great example, or Roy Haynes. There are no pitches at work there.

On the other hand I would make a pretty strong case that, ultimately, Cecil Taylor is a melodic player. The weight of his playing, as interesting as the harmonic stuff is, the rhythmic stuff is, ultimately it's the melodic quality of it that ties it together. It's the glue that makes it all connect and is ultimately a melodic function.

RN: When I spoke to Jack DeJohnette he said, "The dynamics is a melody in itself."

PM: We can continue with that line of thinking too. Harmony is a melody; rhythm is a melody. That's the sort of X-factor aspect of melody; it can transform into any other element at will and back. I think that the best harmonic players and composers include a certain kind of melodic wisdom in each and every movement. The classic example of that would be Bach, right? I mean, you can play any one of his lines and melodically by itself it's more than happening*. It's the absolute greatest melodic step you could ever imagine.

RN: One question I've had trouble getting a straight answer to is: Why is it that one group of notes together will indicate something that is sad and another group of notes will indicate something that's joyous? What's the reason that we have this emotional response to a group of notes? Is it conditioning? Or has it always been there? Is it biological? What do you think, Pat?

PM: I tend to go towards the biological description. Not even biological—physical. That there is in fact a reason why when you examine things on an atomic level you find mathematical relationships that line up almost perfectly with the overtone series. It does seem like on the most minute level of our existence that relationship, the thing that makes a fifth sound good to all of us, exists.

And on the other extreme: From what they seem to be discovering about the way that the universe is moving in space and through time many of the qualities that the

---

* Jazzbos and hipsters such as Metheny and I use the expression "happening" to mean very good, as in "That solo was really happening, Man! Dig?"

overtone series implies appear to work on that level too. So it does seem to be something that's connected on that level.

RN: What you said also made me think about the physical part of it. Obviously each note has a number of vibrations and light is also comprised of vibrations, which is the connection between art and music. Certain combinations of light look to us like red, or whatever, and certain combinations or vibrations of notes sound like A. But it's those combinations that Paul Klee or any other painter puts together in a certain way that resonates with something in you, and that could probably be analyzed by some physicist to always work out to forty-two. That physicist might tell us that all of Klee's paintings, analyzed mathematically would be forty-two and Salvador Dali's paintings would be seventeen. Maybe all of your music analyzed by some scientist would work out to sixty-three. And that's why we all have a different personality in our art. That's sort of related to what you just said.

PM: Let's face it; there are many mysterious aspects to why we all respond to things the way that we generally seem to. My favorite way of describing this is that music is actually this gigantic mistake that we're not actually supposed to know about. That in our sense of the universe around us there's these tiny little cracks that give us a window into everything that we can't possibly understand because we're not equipped to understand those things, because we don't have the tools for them. We don't have the mechanisms to understand them. But somehow music seeps into those cracks and it's something that reminds us or indicates to us these unperceivable things that are in fact around us all the time. I tend to think of music as something that's an incredible variation, away from the rest of most human experiences. For that reason I value it even more.

JACK DeJOHNETTE: The fun thing about playing with Pat is that besides being a deeply committed jazz musician, he's always trying new things—always challenging himself. He has an intense presence in what he does and plays. His vision is to reach a wide audience and he's very successful at doing that, conscientiously using sounds and abstract elements. The spirit of what he does is joyful—seriously joyful! He's relentless in the sense that he always practices a lot and wants to be at his best. You never find Pat "off"!

IMPROVISATION

RN: Let's talk about improvisation itself.

PM: We're improvising most of what we say all the time. At the same time we're using structure, rules, grammar—all of the endless myriad experiences we've had as native English speakers—to put together something that hopefully adds up and makes sense. To me, improvisation in music is almost exactly the same thing.

And we have an array of tools to do that with. And there are some improvisers with a subject to discuss that might be parallel to nuclear physics who need to have an incredibly detailed, complex language that can address the specifics of that subject. On the other hand, you might have some guy who says, "I wanna go to the bar and get drunk!" He has a much smaller need for language. In that sense I'm constantly drawn to the linguistic analogy.

RN: I've always been amazed at how little the public, or even young aspiring musicians, realize how much work goes into

Practicing in the basement of his family's home in 1969

being able to improvise at a high level. They think a guy with your technique wouldn't have to practice. Of course we know it's just the opposite!

PM: The thing you don't read about is just how hard it is. In my case, I was someone who needed to practice a lot. It never came easy for me—especially the physical thing of playing the instrument—and still doesn't! If I don't play for a week or two, it's almost like I've never played. When I have to get ready for a tour, if I haven't been playing for a while, it's excruciating— on a physical level and in all departments. I really envy people who can just pick up their instrument and play it any time. It's just not like that for me.

I went through a stage early on, which was actually of great concern to my parents. I used to practice eight, nine, ten, up to twelve hours a day. I was really determined to find out as much as I could about music. This was during the time when I was supposed to be learning how to read and write! This caused me to be nearly illiterate until much later in life when I started to learn other things.

My love of music is what drives everything. The musicians I've loved the most were those who defined their own voice and had developed an instantly recognizable personal sound.

As much as I love playing on standards and blues forms and modern jazz compositions, there was a way of playing, an improvisational feeling that although I could kind of impose it into that zone a little bit, I didn't find music that really allowed me to follow through on my own improvisational urge.

So I started writing tunes out of necessity. Being a "composer" became a major priority much later, not until my late teens or early twenties. I needed to write material that could launch this way of playing I was interested in. When I was seventeen I wrote a tune called "April Joy" and I consider it the first composition that opened that world to me.

Ultimately, what you're left with is some kind of a sound. At the core of whatever that sound is there has to be a certain kind of truth, a resonance to the person offering that sound that's very, very deep. Unless it has that truth it's really not that difficult to whip up something in the "musical kitchen." But it might not taste that good!

Metheny is often noted for his melodic style and I asked him to demonstrate his approach as it relates to harmony. He used a two-chord framework to show how an improviser can lead the listener's ear to the harmony ("inside") and then progressively away from it ("outside").

PM: So much of the melodic quality I try to invoke in improvisation is really just having clear destinations. I'll play these simple notes.

EXAMPLE 6. *Metheny's notes (© Pat Metheny Music)*

So let's say this implies that the chords are:

EXAMPLE 7. *Metheny's notes (© Pat Metheny Music)*

. . . and I'm going to improvise over that:

EXAMPLE 8. *Metheny's "inside" improvisation (© Pat Metheny Music)*

Somehow even with that, you can still hear the Am to F. Even if the chords aren't there, you just think it. So that's the first sentence you offer to somebody in a conversation. Once you've established that, other notes become possible.

EXAMPLE 9. *Metheny plays some "other notes" (© Pat Metheny Music)*

And when you've established that, then you can get away with anything!

EXAMPLE 10. *Metheny getting away with "anything" (© Pat Metheny Music)*

That was just adding some extra chords, but once you've got that going, you can go anywhere else and add some really weird stuff!

EXAMPLE II. *Metheny adding some "weird stuff"* (© *Pat Metheny Music*)

THE FUTURE

RN: Music: The challenges for the future and the dangers in the present? Discuss.

PM: The challenges for someone starting now are exactly the same as they have always been—but with the additional burden of each decade of new information and innovation that creative artists are required to absorb, or ignore.

It's not easy. The thing we see a lot of now is younger players who are very capable, even exceptional musicians. But they get to a high point of fluency without having much of a story of their own to tell. When I hear many young saxophone players, I have the feeling that there are 500 channels on your cable TV, but there's nothing to watch. There's a lot of stuff, but in terms of someone who can crystallize the feeling of their generation into a language that's unique and their own, and at the same time is addressing all the stuff that they've rightly spent eight or ten years practicing in high school or college, it's odd that there haven't been more musicians who have managed to jump that hurdle.

I also have to say that, on a political level, being original has become less of a goal. Politically we live in an era of Fundamentalism versus Modernism. That's the general conflict in the political world, and in the jazz world the Fundamentalist movement is significant. And that movement makes a case to say that it's OK to sound like Coleman Hawkins, and if you do it great, that's enough. But that's a break from the jazz tradition. Historically, there are few examples where a revisionist view of the world has held sway. I do find the parallels between the political climate and the jazz world fascinating. They mirror each other in many ways.

AFTERWORD

Anyone who devotes a bit of time to thinking about Metheny's last comments, and then factors in the global challenges we face, has every reason to be deeply concerned about the future of creativity in our culture.

On the flip side of those rather alarming concerns, we might also consider that we are indeed fortunate to have lived at a time when artists such as Metheny were allowed to develop and be appreciated and supported by both the artistic and economic environment of the second half of the twentieth century. Our lives have been enriched by them, and we can only suggest to children of the twenty-first century that they open their hearts as these artists offer their sounds and their words. Every note they play and concept they voice is an opportunity to share their optimistic belief that we can and will manifest a better destiny than the present might suggest.

DISCOGRAPHY

Below is a discography of Pat Metheny solo, duo and trio recordings, and Pat Metheny Group albums:

Bright Size Life (1976)

Watercolors (1977)

Pat Metheny Group (1978)

New Chautauqua (1979)

American Garage (1979)

80/81 (1980)

DISCOGRAPHY

As Falls Wichita, So Falls Wichita Falls (1981) with Lyle Mays

Offramp (1982)

Travels (1983)

Rejoicing (1983)

First Circle (1984)

The Falcon and the Snowman (1985)

Song X (1986)

Still Life (Talking) (1987)

Letter from Home (1989)

Question and Answer (1990)

Secret Story (1992)

The Road to You (1993)

DISCOGRAPHY

Zero Tolerance for Silence (1994)

I Can See Your House from Here (1994) with John Scofield

We Live Here (1995)

Quartet (1996)

Passaggio per il Paradiso (1996)

Beyond the Missouri Sky (1997) with Charlie Haden

Imaginary Day (1997)

Like Minds (1999)

Jim Hall and Pat Metheny (1999)

A Map of the World (1999)

Trio (99-00) (2000)

80/81 (2000)

DISCOGRAPHY

Trio Live (2000)

Speaking of Now (2002)

One Quiet Night (2003)

Rarum IX: Selected Recordings (2004)

The Way Up (2005)

The Road to You (2006)

Metheny/Mehldau (2006)

Metheny/Mehldau Quartet (2007)

Day Trip (2008)

INDEX

INDEX

INDEX